# BIRD

Welcoming Wild

Birds to Your Yard

 # GARDENS

Stephen W. Kress Guest Editor

Janet Marinelli
SERIES EDITOR

Jane Ludlam
ACTING MANAGING EDITOR

Bekka Lindstrom
ART DIRECTOR

Stephen K-M. Tim
VICE PRESIDENT, SCIENCE, LIBRARY & PUBLICATIONS

Judith D. Zuk
PRESIDENT

Elizabeth Scholtz
DIRECTOR EMERITUS

Handbook #156

Copyright © Autumn 1998 by the Brooklyn Botanic Garden, Inc.

Handbooks in the *21st-Century Gardening Series,* formerly *Plants & Gardens,*
are published quarterly at 1000 Washington Ave., Brooklyn, NY 11225.

Subscription included in Brooklyn Botanic Garden subscriber membership dues ($35.00 per year).

ISSN # 0362-5850    ISBN # 1-889538-08-6

Printed by Science Press, a division of the Mack Printing Group

Cover photograph: Cedar Waxwing on hawthorn

# Table of Contents

# The Bird-friendly Garden

BY STEPHEN W. KRESS

**M**OST PEOPLE THINK all that's involved in attracting birds to their yards is putting out a feeder or birdbath—but these benefit only a few species and for just short periods of time. Like all plants and animals, birds require specific habitats—for example, open meadows, shrubby gardens, and forest interiors—where specific plants provide food, shelter, nesting spots, and singing posts. Because they are highly mobile, birds move around to find good homes and depart if habitats stop meeting their needs. To attract wild birds throughout the year, gardeners must create and maintain the conditions that a variety of birds favor. Feeders and birdbaths alone will not do the job.

Habitat loss—both in quantity and quality—is the single greatest threat to native land birds. Large forests are increasingly fractured by highways, power lines, and development, allowing predatory edge species, such as grackles and jays, access to the eggs and young of forest-interior birds such as thrushes and tanagers. It is estimated that by the year 2000, about 3.5 million acres in the United States and Canada will be paved for highways and airports and 19.7 million more acres of undeveloped land—an area equivalent in size to the states of Vermont, New Hampshire, Massachusetts, and Rhode Island combined—will be converted to sprawling suburbia.

In this increasingly peopled landscape, bird habitats simply vanish because, in the press to provide housing and services for humans, the needs of wildlife are not considered. Wild birds may be protected by state and federal laws and internation-

Like many birds, the Scarlet Tanager seeks habitats that contain large trees, such as oaks, where it consumes insects, and native shrubs that provide berries.

al treaties that apply to parks and refuges, but the vast majority of land remains in private ownership and has no formal protection. Of the 737 million acres of forested land in the United States, 59 percent is in private, non-industrial ownership, and small landowners decide how to manage these forests, leaving most bird habitats vulnerable to the crush of development.

Protecting and effectively managing large tracts of wild and rural land is the first line of protection for birds—especially forest and grassland species. There is some encouraging news: Programs such as the National Audubon Society's Important Bird Areas and the Nature Conservancy's Last Great Places are actively identifying specific locations that are especially important to birds.

**Although bird habitat is disappearing, gardeners can help counter this trend by creating backyard sanctuaries for hummingbirds and other species.**

Solutions to many of the threats to wild bird populations—habitat loss, acid rain, global warming, agricultural pesticides, and collisions with power lines and skyscrapers—may seem beyond your reach. But you can begin to welcome birds into your own backyard. Plant large trees and native shrubs and vines—the basic elements in a habitat that will benefit generations of wild birds that add color and song to your garden, transforming it into your own mini-wildlife sanctuary. This guide is designed to show you how.

One isolated, bird-friendly backyard in an expanse of mowed suburbia may be of limited benefit to wild birds. But your yard can become the nucleus of a more valuable improvement for birds if, with your neighbors, you can come up with a communal vision and create a series of adjacent bird-friendly backyards, each alive with variety and life. When linked together, such gardens can be meaningful stopovers for migratory songbirds, useful wintering areas, and nesting habitats.

Much of this guide consists of an encyclopedia of plants recommended for attracting birds. All are native species and are included because they provide one or more of the following benefits—food, shelter, or nesting places—and because they are highly decorative and readily available. Add them to your garden, enjoy their color and form, and know that at the same time you are making your little piece of the planet a better place for birds.

THE INTERLACED

# Biology of Birds and Plants

BY STEPHEN W. KRESS

**B**IRDS AND PLANTS have evolved side by side over thousands of years and interact in remarkable ways that often benefit each other. Birds consume the fruits, buds, flowers, and nectar of plants, and as they do so, they pollinate these plants and disperse their seeds over the landscape. In the eastern deciduous forests, at least 300 trees, shrubs, and vines depend solely on birds to spread their seeds—usually far from competing parent plants. Unlike rodents, which destroy seeds by gnawing into the seed coat, birds eat only the fleshy fruit; as the seeds pass through the birds' gizzards they remain intact and the protective seed coat is scarified (scratched)—improving the chances of germination. Bird-distributed seeds also benefit from the high-nitrogen excrement that surrounds seeds when they are "planted."

## Fruit appeal

Plants have, not coincidentally, evolved in ways that assure the appeal of their fruits to their co-conspirators in reproduction. Most trees and shrubs have small fruits, no more than three-fifths of an inch in diameter—just the size of a bird's gape. Many fruits ripen precisely when bird migration reaches its peak. And the majority of plants that depend on birds to distribute their seeds produce brightly colored fruits—again, no coincidence, as birds live in a highly visual world and almost all, with the exception of owls, Whippoorwill, and their kin, have a keen ability to see color.

Plants usually put on their colorful fruit display at the same time that they are producing sugars or fatty lipids, nutrients that serve no purpose for the plant

Birds, like this House Finch, distribute the seeds of plants that produce bright fruits, so it's important to avoid using species that are invasive.

other than enticing flocks of ravenous, seed-dispersing birds; the appearance of brightly colored fruit is an instinctive magnet for fruit-eating birds such as thrushes, catbirds, and waxwings. Some plants deploy bright colors, not in their fruits, but rather in other parts of the plant. Virginia creeper, wild grape, sassafras, and gray dogwood have muted blue or white fruits—but these are either displayed on red stems or ripen just when the leaves attain their most brilliant colors. Virginia creeper and some other vines appear to advertise ripe fruit by prematurely withdrawing chlorophyll from their leaves, revealing red pigments that contrast with the unchanged sea of green foliage around them—at the same time that the vines' fruits ripen and are ready for dispersal.

## Timing is all

In nature, plant fruits ripen in different seasons, providing a nourishing smorgasbord for birds throughout the year. In spring, for example, sweet foods such as serviceberries, wild cherries, mulberries, and strawberries are available to hard-working parent birds. Fall migrants such as thrushes, tanagers, vireos, and warblers require fatty fruits to fuel their long journeys; a few of their favorite fruits are found on spicebush, magnolia, sassafras, and flowering dogwood. The fruits of species such as mountain ash, hawthorn, and cranberrybush viburnum have a low lipid content, making them less desirable to fall migrants—but also less likely to turn rancid and rot on the plants. Some fruits, like nannyberry (wild raisin), shrivel in place and remain available for wintering robins, bluebirds, and flickers. These persistent foods are especially important when late snowfalls cover the ground, preventing returning robins, thrashers, and sparrows from finding earthworms, insects, and other invertebrates under rotting leaves. Likewise, early spring migrants such as the Yellow-rumped Warbler and the Tree Swallow often survive on persistent fruits such as bayberry when spring cold snaps the flying insects on which they typically feed.

## Nourishing natives

Interactions between native birds and native plants have taken thousands of years to evolve. Climate is constantly selecting features of bird behavior and anatomy that fit the habitat—including preferences for specific plant foods. At the same time, plants that are not adept at spreading their seeds are unlikely to

Birds like this Broad-billed Hummingbird pollinate plants as they consume nectar.

survive, as more aggressive species can soon crowd them out. To protect birds and our native plant heritage, gardeners should favor indigenous (native) species and avoid using plants from other areas—especially those that are invasive and have the potential to escape into wild habitats, crowding out native plants. What's more, these non-natives may not provide the proper nutrients. Native plants, which have co-evolved with native wild birds, are more likely to provide a mix of foods—just the right size, and with just the right kind of nutrition—and delivered just when birds need them.

Over the years, some invasive species have been promoted for their benefits to wildlife (see "Invasive Plants to Avoid," page 15). Tartarian

**Tufted Titmouse**

honeysuckle *(Lonicera tatarica)*, for example, is an invasive shrub that has spread so aggressively across the eastern United States that it is crowding out native shrubby dogwoods and viburnums. While this shrub produces prolific orange and red fruits that are readily consumed, monocultures of honeysuckle now replace once-diverse communities of native shrubs, limiting the kinds of foods available throughout the year. A recent study also found that Cedar Waxwing that feed on tartarian honeysuckle often have orange-tipped rather than yellow-tipped tail feathers. Plumage colors are badges used for gender and species recognition, so the effects of food on birds' color could be very disruptive.

Much remains to be learned about the interactions between birds and plants—even the feeding habits of common birds are not well understood. But if you watch the birds that visit your yard carefully, you will see that they use a wide range of plants for feeding, resting, and shelter—and likewise that many, many plants rely on birds to distribute their seeds. These relationships between birds and plants reflect thousands of years of co-evolution and are dynamic and changing. In light of these complex interactions, our attempts to create bird habitats can be humbling, but—when successful—immensely satisfying.

☒

12 WAYS TO

# Design a
# Bird-friendly
# Garden

BY STEPHEN W. KRESS

**B**EFORE YOU BEGIN designing your bird garden, be sure to visit several nearby natural areas, such as parks and wildlife sanctuaries. These will give you a sense of what kinds of plants and plant communities make up the natural bird habitat in your area. Take notes on what species grow in these natural places and how the plant communities are structured—how they form vertical layers, for example, and how some plants occur in large drifts. Re-creating a similar type of growth using species native to your area is the key to a successful bird garden.

Once you've gotten a sense of the structure and makeup of the local bird habitat, make a drawing of your property and its perimeter, and sketch in all of your existing plants, especially trees and shrubs. Also note the herbaceous plants that benefit birds, such as pokeberry *(Phytolacca americana)* and black-eyed Susans *(Rudbeckia* species). Sketch in your house, outbuildings, driveway, and other primary features. With this map in hand, you'll be able to identify the resources you already have for attracting birds; you should protect and nurture these. You can also use this sketch to plan additional plantings appropriate for your area.

Following are 12 general guidelines on how to design a garden that appeals to both birds and people. For specific plant recommendations organized by region, see the encyclopedia section starting on page 25.

## 1. Re-create the layers of plant growth found in local natural areas.

All natural areas are composed of various layers of plant growth. In the deciduous forests of the Northeast, for example, dominant trees such as sugar maple and American beech form a high canopy above an understory of intermediate-sized trees such as hornbeam and serviceberry. Below this is a layer of tall shrubs such as spicebush and witchhazel, then smaller shrubs such as fragrant sumac and mapleleaf viburnum, and finally groundcovers such as partridgeberry and mosses. The layers are intertwined with vines such as Virginia creeper and wild grape. The forest edge is also layered, but with different plants, including dogwoods, nannyberry, and arrowwood.

Mimic layers of the local flora when creating your garden.

Birds use most or all of these various layers for a multitude of purposes. The Wood Thrush, for instance, usually sings from the highest trees—those that form the canopy. They build their nests in the layer of tall shrubs below, and find food by scratching through leaf litter. Their nests include material from all of the layers, including mud, leaves, and grapevine bark.

Be sure to mimic the vertical layers of nearby native plant communities when designing your bird garden. A handy rule of thumb is to plant tall forest-interior trees along the periphery of your property; a bit closer to the house, plant understory trees, then large shrubs, small shrubs, and, closer still, groundcovers such as bunch grasses and wildflowers. Once these plantings are well established, plant or encourage the growth of vines. If your garden already has large trees, establish islands of variable-height plantings around them.

A lawn doesn't feed or shelter birds.

Birds of open habitats such as meadows and prairies require many acres of grassland, but you will have some success attracting Bobolink, meadowlarks, and Savannah Sparrow to your yard by keeping the lawn in grass and planting a few shrubs that the birds will use as singing posts.

## 2. Select plants with an eye to providing nutritional foods during different seasons.

Different birds require different kinds of foods in different seasons. During the rigorous chick-rearing days, for example, parent birds get the energy they need by feeding on sweet fruits such as blackberries, mulberries, and wild cherries. Fall migrants (thrushes, vireos, and warblers) require fatty fruits such as flowering dog-

Northern Cardinal needs fruit in winter.

wood, spicebush, and mapleleaf viburnum to build fat reserves for their long journey, while wintering birds (finches, sparrows, and waxwings) need abundant, persistent fruits such as those of conifers, bayberry, hawthorns, crabapples, and sumacs to help them survive subfreezing temperatures. Such persistent fruits are also extremely important for early spring migrants such as bluebirds, robins, and thrashers. Be sure to include a variety of plants that can help sustain the various birds that visit your garden year round.

## 3. Plant small trees and shrubs in same-species clumps.

This is necessary for pollination of dioecious shrubs such as hollies and mulberries, with separate male and female plants. Even for species with flowers of both sexes on the same plant, planting in clumps helps boost fertility and therefore fruit yields. Clumps also benefit birds by providing highly visible, massed displays of fruit. To create a natural look, avoid planting trees and shrubs in rows, and for aesthetic reasons, plant odd numbers of specimens in rounded patches to reduce the goal-post look or plantation effect that can otherwise result.

## 4. Provide at least one clump of conifers.

Birds find shelter in evergreen conifers during storms and winter weather. They also are preferred roosting (sleeping) and nesting sites.

## 5. Spare a dead tree (snag) for the birds.

Birds tend to perch in dead trees, which they use as singing posts to defend their territories. It's also a good idea to leave a few dead branches on live trees for perches. Woodpeckers will channel out nesting cavities in the soft wood of dead trees and use the trees for drumming—the woodpecker substitute for territorial song. Dead trees also make excellent anchors for bird houses.

## 6. Leave vines or plant them.

Vines such as Virginia creeper, greenbrier, and poison ivy provide birds with perches, nesting places, and leaf surfaces from which insect-eaters such as warblers and kinglets can glean good, abundant fruit crops. Wild grape, another vine popular among birds, provides food for at least 51 species of birds, and at least 16 species use the stringy bark to help build their nests.

Plant vines such as Virginia creeper.

## 7. Limit the size of your lawn.

A manicured lawn doesn't provide much in the way of food or habitat for birds, and typically contributes to a host of other environmental problems associated with fertilizing, mowing, and the use of pesticides to control insects and diseases. Across the country, people are experimenting with changing the composition of their yards and introducing native species. They are gradually replacing the monotonous green of the lawn with more natural plant communities closely mimicking the prairies or woodlands that existed before suburbia altered the American landscape. Such habitats are more interesting and much kinder to backyard birds.

*continues on page 16*

# INVASIVE PLANTS TO AVOID

Following is a list of some of the most invasive non-native species, which could mistakenly be planted to benefit birds. Avoid planting them. If you already have some of these species growing in your yard, remove them so that they won't spread further.

For a comprehensive list of invasive plants used in gardens, as well as a guide to identification and control, consult Brooklyn Botanic Garden handbook #149, *Invasive Plants: Weeds of the Global Garden* (to order, see page 112).

| Species | Where invasive |
|---|---|
| Norway Maple *(Acer platanoides)* | Northeast |
| Australian Pine *(Casuarina equisetifolia)* | South Florida |
| Edible Fig *(Ficus carica)* | Pacific Coast |
| Melaleuca *(Melaleuca quinquenervia)* | Southeast & South Florida |
| Chinaberry Tree *(Melia azedarach)* | Southeast |
| Chinese Tallow Tree *(Sapium sebiferum)* | Southeast |
| Japanese Barberry *(Berberis thunbergii)* | Northeast |
| Scotch Broom *(Cystisus scoparius)* | Pacific Coast |
| Russian Olive *(Elaeagnus angustifolia)* | Prairies, Mountains & Northeast |
| Autumn Olive *(Elaeagnus umbellata)* | Northeast & Southeast |
| Chinese Privet *(Ligusticum vulgare)* | Northeast & Southeast |
| Cotoneasters *(Cotoneaster* species) | Pacific Coast |
| Japanese Privet *(Ligustrum japonicum)* | Northeast & Southeast |
| Bush Honeysuckles *(Lonicera maackii,* | Pacific Coast, Northeast & |
| L. morrowii, and L. tatarica) | Southeast |
| Japanese Honeysuckle *(Lonicera japonica)* | Northeast & Southeast |
| European Buckthorn *(Rhamnus cathartica)* | Northeast & Prairies |
| Glossy Buckthorn *(Rhamnus frangula)* | Northeast & Prairies |
| Multiflora Rose *(Rosa multiflora)* | Northeast & Southeast |
| Brazilian Pepper *(Schinus terebinthifolius)* | Southeast & South Florida |
| Porcelain Berry *(Ampelopsis brevipedunculata)* | Northeast |
| Oriental Bittersweet *(Celastrus orbiculatus)* | Northeast |
| Leafy Spurge *(Euphorbia esula)* | Prairies |
| Purple Loosestrife *(Lythrum salicaria)* | Northeast & Southeast |
| White Mulberry *(Morus alba)* | Northeast, Southeast & Pacific Coast |

Invasive non-natives, such as the cotoneaster in this California garden, crowd out the diverse mixes of native plants most beneficial to birds.

Many people feel that grass is an essential play surface for children; if you plan to include lawn in your yard, seek out the kinds of grasses that require little upkeep and that stand up well to children, too. As your children grow, you can reduce the area dedicated to grass, replacing it with other low-maintenance plants, including native wildflowers and grasses, and shrubs and woodland groundcovers.

**8. Avoid invasive non-native plants.**

Invasive non-native plants are still commonly available through many nurseries, in part because some provide food and cover for wildlife (see the box on page 15). However, the threats of these plants to native vegetation and wildlife far outweigh any short-term benefits. They can rapidly invade natural areas, crowding out diverse mixes of native plants that are much more valuable to wildlife. Others pose a threat to the unique gene pools of closely related natives, as white (Russian) mulberry *(Morus alba)* threatens red mulberry *(M. rubra)* by interbreeding.

**9. Supply a source of water.**

Birds get much of the water they need from foods, but they will readily use open water sources for drinking and bathing. Birds in arid regions such as mountains and deserts are especially drawn to such watering spots, but birds in the Northeast, Southeast, and Pacific coastal regions are also highly attracted to open water year-round. Birds need water not only for drinking but also to cool themselves in the heat of the summer, while wintering birds welcome water when natural supplies become locked in ice and snow and are unavailable.

During migration, land birds are most in need of fresh water. Each spring many perform a remarkable feat, flying nonstop over the Gulf of Mexico,

*continues on page 20*

Provide a shallow source of water for birds such as these splashing House Finch.

## PESTICIDES AND BACKYARD BIRDS

Pesticides are a threat to insect-eating birds like this Eastern Bluebird.

After World War II, DDT and other organochlorine pesticides developed during the war quickly became the primary weapons against pests. After two decades of heavy use, researchers found that DDT and related organochlorine pesticides aldrin/dieldrin and chlordane/heptachlor seriously interfered with the reproductive capacity of several raptors, notably the Bald Eagle, Osprey, and Peregrine Falcon. The shells of these raptors' eggs became so thin that the birds could not survive.

In her revolutionary book, *Silent Spring,* published in the early 1960s, Rachel Carson called the world's attention to the impact of pesticides on birds and their potential harm to humans. By 1972, DDT was banned by the U.S. Environmental Protection Agency, which soon after banned aldrin/dieldrin and chlordane/heptachlor. In their place, organophosphate pesticides came into use. This family of nerve poisons was developed for military use, but researchers soon discovered the value of these chemicals as pesticides. Although they have less residual effect than the organochlorines, meaning they break down more readily in the environment, organophosphates are very toxic at small doses. Humans can protect themselves when applying the pesticides or re-entering sprayed fields by donning protective clothing, gloves, and boots, and by using respirators. Unfortunately, birds cannot protect themselves, and many organophosphates widely used as agricultural pesticides (notably fenthion, diazinon, and carbofuran) have killed birds by the thousands.

Pesticide use in homes and gardens has increased since the 1980s, in part because of the growth of the commercial lawn-care business. Nearly 5,000 lawn-care firms serve nearly 12 percent of all households with private lawns. Many of these companies apply pesticides and fertilizers according to a calendar, rather than by monitoring pest levels on their clients' properties and responding accordingly.

Whether on your lawn or in other parts of your garden, use chemical pesticides (if you must use them at all) only as a last resort, after all other measures have failed. Use them judiciously, following all instructions on the label. The following pesticides have had a particularly adverse impact on birds:

*Organophosphates to avoid:*

**Furadan (Carbofuran)**—An insecticide and nematicide available in granular or liquid formulations. Birds that ingest a grain of Furadan, mistaking it for seed, die almost immediately. Liquid formulations have also been responsible for the deaths of many species of migratory birds.

**Spectracide (Diazinon)**—A broad-spectrum insecticide applied in granular or liquid form that is highly toxic to waterfowl and other birds. After dramatic bird kills in the 1980s, the use of diazinon was prohibited on all sod farms and golf courses, but it is still sold for home use. Birds are poisoned when they eat grass, grass roots, or grass seed of turf that has been treated with this pesticide, or any worms or insects in the grass.

**Dursban (Chlorpyrifos)**—An insecticide widely used for termites and household and garden pests that is toxic to young birds.

*Organochlorines to avoid:*

**Kelthane (Dicofol)**—A miticide used on turf and shrubs, which has been implicated in the deaths of Peregrine Falcon that ate insects killed by the formulation.

*—Maureen Kuwano Hinkle*

exhausting both their fat and water supplies; they must refuel and rehydrate at the first opportunity in coastal states.

Hummingbirds sometimes bathe in a few drops of water that collect in the midribs of large leaves, but most land birds prefer to drink and bathe in shallow puddles and pools, and will readily use bird baths. Baths atop pedestals will keep birds out of reach of predatory cats and are easier to clean than ground-level baths. When choosing a bath, find one with a shallow slope, as most birds are short-legged and avoid deep water.

Clean the bath with a stiff brush every few days in summer, adding water as needed; make sure that it is no deeper than three inches at the deepest spots. Make sure, too, that the water is clean, as birds will drink from your bath as well as bathe, and excrement and algae can accumulate when baths are neglected. Birds are especially attracted to pools that have a dripping action; they like to perch on the source of the drip and drink drops of water before they fall into the pool. Birds are probably lured to these baths by the movement of the dripping water and the concentric ripples created as each drop falls. Several devices are available that tap into garden hose supplies to create a continuous dripping action.

Birds bathe and drink in winter as well as summer, so make sure that your bath does not freeze over completely during cold weather. When the air temperature hovers just below freezing, add warm water to the bath several times a day. At lower temperatures, you will need to install an electric heating device to provide a reliable water source. Cement or granite birdbaths are best for winter use because ceramic baths can crack when water freezes.

Birds are also attracted to larger garden pools. For details on how to create a water garden that can double as bird habitat, consult Brooklyn Botanic Garden handbook # 151, *The Natural Water Garden: Pools, Ponds, Marshes, and Bogs for Backyards Everywhere* (to order, see page 112).

### 10. Provide nest boxes.

Birds that nest in tree cavities often lack suitable nesting places, as natural cavities are scarce; these cavities develop when branches break off and the wound does not self-heal, permitting the inner wood to rot. Most cavity-nesting birds rely on woodpeckers to create their nesting and roosting places. Woodpeckers chisel into trees to feed, creating openings that are often enlarged for nesting by small cavity nesters like chickadees and titmice. Squirrels and larger birds such as the Great-crested Flycatcher may enlarge these holes further. Suitably sized cavities have probably always been scarce, but they are in even greater demand

*continues on page 24*

A nest box provides a post for both an Eastern Bluebird and a Virginia creeper vine.

# Building Nest Boxes

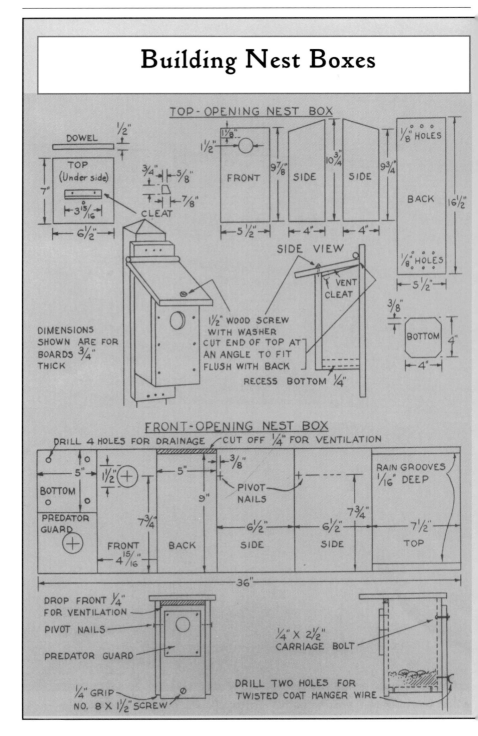

The size of both a nest box itself and the entrance is crucial in determining which birds use it. If you wish to attract a specific bird species to your nest box, modify these plans by following the recommended sizes listed below. When building a nest box, make sure you match each edge to its corresponding edge as shown at left. Nail the sides to the base, then attach the back, the front, and finally the roof. The nest box should be treated with a nontoxic wood preservative.

## NEST BOX DIMENSIONS

| SPECIES | FLOOR (IN.) | CHIPS | DEPTH (IN.) | ENTRANCE ABOVE FLOOR (IN.) | DIAMETER OF ENTRANCE (IN.) | HEIGHT (FT) ABOVE GROUND OR WATER (W) | PREFERRED HABITAT CODES§ |
|---|---|---|---|---|---|---|---|
| Wood Duck | 12x12 | + | 22 | 17 | 4 | 20–10,6W | 3,5 |
| Hooded Merganser | 10x10 | + | 15–18 | 10–13 | 5 | 4–6 | 3,5 |
| American Kestrel | 8x8 | + | 12–15 | 9–12 | 3 | 10–30 | 1,4 |
| Barn Owl | 10x18 | + | 15–18 | 0–4 | 6 | 12–18 | 4 |
| Barred Owl | 12x12 | + | 20–24 | 14 | 6x6 | 15–20 | 5 |
| Screech Owl | 8x8 | + | 12–15 | 9–12 | 3 | 10–30 | 2 |
| Golden-fronted Woodpecker | 6x6 | + | 12 | 9 | 2 | 10–20 | 2 |
| Downy Woodpecker | 4x4 | + | 9 | 7 | 1¼ | 5–15 | 2 |
| Northern Flicker | 7x7 | + | 16–18 | 14–16 | 2½ | 6–30 | 1,2 |
| Great crested Flycatcher | 6x6 | + | 8–10 | 6–8 | $1\frac{9}{16}$* | 8–20 | 1,2 |
| Ash-throated Flycatcher | 6x6 | + | 8–10 | 6–8 | 1½* | 8–20 | 1,6 |
| Purple Martin | 6x6 | – | 6 | 1 | 2¼ | 10–20 | 1 |
| Tree Swallow | 5x5 | – | 6–8 | 4–6 | 1½* | 4–15 | 1 |
| Violet-green Swallow | 5x5 | – | 6–8 | 4–6 | 1½* | 4–15 | 1 |
| Chickadees | 4x4 | + | 9 | 7 | 1⅛ | 4–15 | 2 |
| Titmouse | 4x4 | + | 9 | 7 | 1¼ | 5–15 | 2 |
| Nuthatches | 4x4 | + | 9 | 7 | 1⅜ | 5–15 | 2 |
| Carolina Wren | 4x4 | – | 6–8 | 4–6 | 1½* | 5–10 | 2,7 |
| Bewick's Wren | 4x4 | – | 6–8 | 4–6 | 1¼ | 5–10 | 2,7 |
| House Wren | 4x4 | – | 6–8 | 4–6 | 1–1¼ | 4–10 | 2,7 |
| Bluebird (Eastern, Western) | 4x4 | – | 8–12 | 6–10 | 1½* | 3–6 | 1 |
| Mountain Bluebird | 4x4 | – | 8–12 | 6–10 | $1\frac{9}{16}$* | 3–6 | 1 |

*Precise measurement required; if diameter is larger, starlings may usurp cavity.
§Preferred habitat codes: **1.** Open areas in the sun (not shaded permanently by trees), pastures, fields, or golf courses. **2.** Woodland clearings or the edge of woods. **3.** Above water, or if on land, the entrance should face water. **4.** On trunks of large trees, or high in little-frequented parts of barns, silos, water towers, or church steeples. **5.** Moist forest bottomlands, flooded river valleys, swamps. **6.** Semiarid country, deserts, dry open woods, and wood edge. **7.** Backyards, near buildings. **8.** Near water; under bridges, barns. **9.** Mixed conifer-hardwood forests.

Chart adapted from Daniel D. Boone, *Homes for Birds.* Conservation Bulletin 14, 1979, 22 pp.; also Susan E. Quinlan, *Bird Houses for Alaska*, vol. 1, no. 3, Alaska Wildlife Watcher's Report, Alaska Department of Fish and Game, 1982, 8 pp.

Illustration from Stephen W. Kress, *The Audubon Society Guide to Attracting Birds,* Charles Scribner's Sons, 1985. Reprinted with the author's permission.

today because native birds are competing with House Sparrow and European Starling, which usurp millions of nesting places that traditionally would have been used by the native bird life.

The simplest way to increase the variety of birds nesting on your property is to provide nest boxes, which substitute for natural tree cavities. In all, 48 species are known to raise young in nest boxes, including bluebirds, Tree Swallow, Purple Martin, and Prothonotary Warbler. Some species prefer wood chips in the bottom of their nest box to cradle eggs, while others build elaborate nests of sticks, grass, and feathers. Boxes can be made of any wood, but avoid using wood preservatives and paint on the interior, as these could affect the eggs or young. There are a variety of excellent designs for boxes, but they must include a sloping roof to shed rain, drainage holes in the bottom, an access door for annual late-winter cleaning, and a predator guard to keep raccoons from reaching in to snatch eggs and young. By keeping the entrance hole 1½ inches in diameter or smaller, you can exclude starlings. Modify the box dimensions and size of the openings to accommodate specific species (see drawing, page 22).

Location is another important consideration. Bluebird houses placed in the woods will be used by chickadees and titmice; if placed at the forest edge or in thickets, expect to find House Wren. However, place the same box in an open field and you'll likely attract bluebirds or Tree Swallow.

### 11. Leave some leaf litter for the birds.

Rather than raking leaves into a pile for roadside pick-up, use them to create feeding places for ground-feeding birds such as thrashers, White-throated Sparrow, and robins and other thrushes. Just rake the leaves under hedges or trees that produce a dense shade. Rake the leaves in the fall, creating beds five to six inches thick; by spring, they will have decomposed just enough to have attracted a good supply of earthworms, insects,and other animals on which the birds feed.

### 12. Use pesticides sparingly, if at all.

Some pesticides harm birds directly (see the box on page 18). Others kill or contaminate insects and other creatures on which many birds feed.

Keep in mind that the typical lawn is coddled with an arsenal of chemicals. If you're thinking of hiring a lawn-care company, choose one that favors the use of alternatives to chemical insecticides and herbicides. If they do recommend the use of chemicals, ask for the names of the substances, the reasons for their use, the quantities to be applied, and where and when it will be done.

# Bird-Attracting Plants

O n the following pages, you'll find 72 great garden plants for birds, a dozen for every major region: the Northeast, the Southeast, South Florida, the prairies and plains, the western mountains and deserts, and the Pacific Coast (see the map on page 106). Five national authorities on wild birds selected the plants, species native to North America that benefit birds by providing not only food, but also shelter and nesting places. For each region, you'll also find a list of additional recommended plants, which in most cases are as valuable to the birds and in the garden as the main selections.

**NORTHEAST**

# The Northeast

BY STEPHEN W. KRESS

*Acer saccharum*
**SUGAR MAPLE**
When mature, these stately, impressive trees have grand trunks, broad, spreading branches, and a symmetrical shape, and grow up to 70'. Many birds find nesting spots in the branches and tree cavities and dine on the seeds, buds, and even the sap.
**NATIVE HABITAT:** Rich, deep, well-drained soils of upland forests.
**USDA HARDINESS ZONES:** 4 to 8
**FLOWERS AND FRUIT:** Flowers are small, bright yellow, and appear April to June with the leaves; fruits are paired, winged seeds that ripen mid-September to October and often persist into winter. Fruits first appear when trees are about 40 years old; trees bear heavy crops every 3 to 7 years, and light crops in intervening years.
**HOW TO GROW:** Sugar maples are best planted as balled and burlapped specimens in early spring or fall. They grow about 1' per year for the first 30 to 40 years. Because they are slow to mature, they will not reach their full stature for wildlife in your time—but they will live for 200 to 300 years—and benefit wildlife for generations. They grow best in rich, deep soils and thrive where

Sugar maple (*Acer saccharum*)

they have clean air and are safe from road salt. Plant as specimen trees in an open area or in a grove; their brilliant fall colors and arching form make them ideal as an entrance promenade.
**BIRDS ATTRACTED:** Branches provide ideal nesting places for the American Robin, Red-eyed Vireo, Northern Oriole, and Rose-breasted Grosbeak; tree cavities are popular nesting places for Screech Owl, woodpeckers, and other cavity nesters; seeds and buds are favorites of the Evening Grosbeak, and the seeds are eaten by Pine Grosbeak,

Rose-breasted Grosbeak, and Northern Cardinal. Many species sip the sweet sap that sometimes drips from wounds in spring.

**ALTERNATIVES:** Box elder *(Acer negundo)* and red maple *(Acer rubrum)* also produce seeds favored by grosbeaks, but these smaller maples are shorter lived and provide fewer nesting sites when mature.

Shadbush *(Amelanchier canadensis)*

## *Amelanchier canadensis*
### SHADBUSH, SERVICEBERRY

Shadbush fruits feed at least two dozen bird species and provide nesting spots for others. Usually a many-stemmed shrub, shadbush may also occur as a small tree to 25'. This is the most abundant shadbush both in the wild and in nurseries.

**NATIVE HABITAT:** Forest edges and understories.

**USDA HARDINESS ZONES:** 5 to 7

**FLOWERS AND FRUIT:** Named for the clustered white blossoms with long, graceful petals that appear in the Northeast when shad (herring-like fish) are migrating up streams (March to June), often around Easter (hence its other common name, serviceberry). Fruits are dark purple, about ⅓" long, and sweet enough for use in pies and jellies. Fruits appear in June to August and are quickly eaten by birds.

**HOW TO GROW:** Shadbush is readily available at most nurseries, with its root mass wrapped in burlap. Plant in early spring to give roots maximum time to grow before the heat of summer; plants tolerate some shade and grow in well-drained, moist, or wet soils. Water frequently, especially in the first year following planting. Plant in front of pine or hemlock for a dramatic spring flowering effect.

**BIRDS ATTRACTED:** At least 26 species are known to eat shadbush fruit, including Hairy Woodpecker, Brown Thrasher, Eastern Bluebird, Cedar Waxwing, Purple Finch, Scarlet Tanager, and Rose-breasted Grosbeak. Kingbirds, American Robin, and Wood Thrush use shadbush for nesting.

**ALTERNATIVES:** Other good choices include downy serviceberry *(Amelanchier arborea)*, often a small tree, although it may grow as a shrub. Some tree forms have a trunk diameter of 8"

**NORTHEAST**

to 16". Running serviceberry *(A. stolonifera)* is a low-growing shrub 2' to 4' tall that likes sun or part shade and thrives in a variety of soil types.

---

*Celastrus scandens*
## AMERICAN BITTERSWEET

American bittersweet, a native species, has been cultivated from the wild since 1736. This vigorous vine has thornless, brown stems and can climb to 60'. More than a dozen bird species consume the bright red and orange fruits, which are festive in color and brighten the landscape.

**NATIVE HABITAT:** Well-drained sites in woods and fencerows.

**USDA HARDINESS ZONES:** 2 to 8

**FLOWERS AND FRUIT:** Insignificant green flowers appear May to June; fruits first ripen in August and remain on the vines to December or later; they are most attractive in late fall and early winter when the fruits burst open, exposing the red interiors.

**HOW TO GROW:** Male and female plants should be placed closely together to facilitate pollination. Vines spread rapidly over the ground and can be used to reduce erosion. Prune regularly to prevent too rampant growth. Plant on a trellis, stone wall, or a fence. Place this favorite ornamental plant where its bright fruits will show off nicely against the snow.

**BIRDS ATTRACTED:** At least 15 species

American bittersweet

are known to eat bittersweet, including Northern Mockingbird, Eastern Bluebird, Red-eyed Vireo, Northern Cardinal, and Pine Grosbeak.

**ALTERNATIVES:** Caution!—Oriental bittersweet *(Celastrus orbiculatus)* looks similar to American bittersweet, but is invasive in more than 20 states in open woods, thickets, and roadsides, and should not be planted.

---

*Cornus florida*
## FLOWERING DOGWOOD

More than 100 bird species are known to eat the fruit of this lovely small tree.

**NATIVE HABITAT:** Moist, rich, well-drained soils along forest borders, near streams, or on south-facing slopes.

**USDA HARDINESS ZONES:** 5 to 8

**FLOWERS AND FRUIT:** "Blooms" consist of four white bracts that appear March to June; some cultivars have pink bracts, but white dogwoods are more vigorous. Scarlet, oval drupes form in clusters that ripen from August to November. The fruits have a high lipid content, which makes them very desirable to fall migrants.

**HOW TO GROW:** Large specimens may be purchased balled and burlapped at most nurseries. Plant trees either in early spring or early fall; they tolerate partial shade, but do best in sun, and prefer soils with a pH range of 6 to 7. Flowering dogwood is susceptible to dogwood anthracnose, but this is less of a problem for trees that are well watered during drought, mulched adequately, and pruned of diseased wood. (A helpful publication on anthracnose is *How to Identify and Control Dogwood Anthracnose.* Manfred E. Mielke and Margery L. Daughtrey. NA-GR-18. Available from USDA Forest Service NA, State and Private Forestry, 5 Radnor Corp. Center, Suite 200, 100 Matsonford Rd., P.O. Box 6775, Radnor, PA 19087.)

**BIRDS ATTRACTED:** Flowering dogwood fruits are a preferred food of Northern Flicker, Pileated Woodpecker, Northern Mockingbird, American Robin, Wood Thrush, Hermit Thrush, Eastern Bluebird, Summer Tanager, Northern Cardinal, Evening Grosbeak, and many others.

**ALTERNATIVES:** Kousa dogwood is often recommended by horticulturists as an alternative to flowering dogwood, as it is relatively resistant to dogwood anthracnose, but this native of Korea produces large red fruits that are too big for most birds to swallow. Try alternate-leaved dogwood, *Cornus alternifolia*, instead.

Flowering dogwood (*Cornus florida*)

*Cornus racemosa*
## GRAY DOGWOOD, PANICLED DOGWOOD

This dense, upright shrub, to 6' tall, is an excellent choice for creating dense patches of cover and food for birds.

**NATIVE HABITAT:** Dry upland thickets, forest borders, and hedgerows.

**USDA HARDINESS ZONES:** 5 to 7

**FLOWERS AND FRUIT:** From May to July, small white flowers appear in loose clumps, about 2" in diameter. Fruits are round white drupes on bright red stems; they ripen July to October and

NORTHEAST

Gray dogwood (*Cornus racemosa*) is a good choice for city bird gardens.

persist after leaves fall into early winter; leaves turn burgundy red in the fall when fruits are ripe.

**HOW TO GROW:** Use this hardy dogwood to create thickets along fencerows or property borders. The plants are slow growing and reach their mature size in about 10 years. They can withstand city growing conditions. Plants can be purchased from nurseries and planted in early spring or fall; they can also be propagated from root cuttings.

**BIRDS ATTRACTED:** At least 16 species are known to eat the fruits of gray dogwood. They are especially preferred by Wild Turkey, Northern Flicker, Downy Woodpecker, Gray Catbird, Swainson's Thrush, Cedar Waxwing, Northern Cardinal, and Pine Grosbeak. Small birds find cover in the dense growth and catbirds often build their nests in it.

**ALTERNATIVES:** Clump-forming dogwoods can be grown together to create borders and thickets that offer food, shelter, and nesting places. Red-osier dogwood *(Cornus stolonifera)* is similar to gray dogwood with white fruit, but has bright red (or yellow) stems and greater tolerance for moist soils; silky dogwood *(Cornus amomum),* grows 4' to 10' tall with full clusters of cobalt blue drupes that are readily eaten by many birds. Bunchberry *(Cornus canadensis)* is a groundcover, growing to just 5" to 12" tall with a large white flower and a cluster of bright red drupes.

*Ilex verticillata*
**WINTERBERRY**
Winterberry's scarlet fruits persist well into winter, giving the plant its name

and feeding a dozen or more bird species. This highly decorative plant brightens the landscape, especially against early snow. The many-stemmed shrub grows 5' to 15' tall.

**NATIVE HABITAT:** Wet soils near swamps, ponds, and wet woods.

**USDA HARDINESS ZONES:** 4 to 7

**FLOWERS AND FRUIT:** Small, greenish white flowers appear April to July on separate male and female plants. Fruiting period is August to October, persisting into winter after leaves fall; fruits are bright scarlet drupes about ¼" in diameter.

**HOW TO GROW:** A good choice for moist, wet soils. Plant several together to form a clump or hedge for best effect and to insure ample pollination. Grows well in full sun and partial shade. Excellent as a border to naturalize pond edges along with elderberry and red-osier dogwood.

**BIRDS ATTRACTED:** At least 12 species eat winterberry fruits. It is preferred by Northern Mockingbird, Gray Catbird, Brown Thrasher, and Hermit Thrush and is used for nesting by Cedar Waxwing and Red-winged Blackbird.

**ALTERNATIVES:** Smooth winterberry *(Ilex laevigata)* is similar to common winterberry, but its leaves are narrower and it grows taller—10' to 20'. The fruits are larger, but not as winter-persistent. It grows from southern Maine to Georgia. Inkberry *(Ilex glabra)*

grows 6' to 10' with black, shiny fruits. It does well in garden settings, tolerating shady, dry, and windy locations. American holly *(Ilex opaca)* is the largest native holly. It has a compact form and evergreen leaves, often growing to 40'. Like other hollies, it has male and female plants, so multiple plantings are necessary for the females to produce their crops of bright red fruit. It is hardy north to Zone 5.

---

## *Lindera benzoin*
### COMMON SPICEBUSH

Fall migrants favor the fruits of this spreading shrub, which grows in damp forest soils and along streams. It is shade-tolerant, but also thrives in areas where it receives sunlight.

**NATIVE HABITAT:** Understories in moist forests.

**USDA HARDINESS ZONES:** 5 to 8

**FLOWERS AND FRUIT:** Clusters of bright yellow flowers appear March to May in the axils of the previous year's leaves. Flowers appear before leaves. Fruits are ½"-long, bright red drupes that occur singly or in clusters along the stem; they ripen July to October, but are quickly eaten by birds. The fruits have a high fat content that makes them highly favored by fall migrants.

**HOW TO GROW:** Spicebush is an excellent planting for borders or foundation plantings on the north side of homes, or as an addition to understory plantings. This spreading shrub grows to 15', with a spread of 2' to 8'. Its spring blooms, fragrant leaves, fall fruits, and bright yellow foliage make it a delightful landscaping choice. It can be propagated from September cuttings of shoots.

BIRDS ATTRACTED: The fruits are eaten by at least 15 species including Great-crested Flycatcher, Gray Catbird, American Robin, and Red-eyed Vireo. It is a preferred food for Wood Thrush and Veery.

ALTERNATIVES: Witchhazel *(Hamamelis virginiana)* and mapleleaf viburnum *(Viburnum acerifolium)* can grow in similar habitats.

---

*Pinus strobus*
## WHITE PINE
In the forest, white pine may grow to a stately 100', with plume-like, horizontal branches. In full sun, trees are often smaller and have a dense structure (especially when pruned), which provides excellent cover for birds. Dozens of species consume the seeds.

NATIVE HABITAT: Dry plateaus to wet swamps.

USDA HARDINESS ZONES: 4 to 7

FLOWERS AND FRUIT: In April to June, tiny female cones appear, which mature by August to September. Cones first appear on 10-year-old trees; heavy crops usually occur when the trees are 20 years old. Seeds occur in 4"- to 8"-long cones that fall in winter or spring.

HOW TO GROW: White pine is naturally adaptable, making it an ideal landscaping plant. Trees are easily transplanted when young as they have shallow roots, and may grow 1' or more each year. They do best in full sun and prefer moist, sandy loam soils. Longer branches often break off when snow builds up, but the trees can live for several hundred years.

BIRDS ATTRACTED: At least 48 species are known to eat the seeds or to find cover or nesting places in the branches. The seeds are a preferred food for Wild

White pine (*Pinus strobus*)

Turkey, Mourning Dove, Red-bellied Woodpecker, Black-capped Chickadee, White-breasted Nuthatch, Brown Creeper, Pine Warbler, Evening Grosbeak, Pine Siskin, Red Crossbill, and many others. Many species also use older trees and snags for cavity nesting.

**ALTERNATIVES:** Pitch pine *(Pinus rigida)* grows on sandy soils, attaining heights of 40' to 60' and is also a good source of seed and usually provides good cover and nesting cavities. Red pine *(Pinus resinosa)* is very hardy (to Zone 3) and grows in poor soils, providing heavy seed crops every 3 to 7 years.

---

## Rhus typhina
### STAGHORN SUMAC

The fruits of this shrub or small tree feed at least 31 species of birds, which also consume the fruits of other sumacs. Staghorn sumac spreads by root sprouts to create a circular clone in a dense clump.

**NATIVE HABITAT:** Hedgerows, roadsides, and woodland borders on well-drained soils.

**USDA HARDINESS ZONES:** 4 to 8

**FLOWERS AND FRUIT:** Tiny yellow-green flowers appear May to July in distinct, fragrant spikes. Small, hairy, bright red drupes ripen August to September, in compact clusters of 700 or more that persist on the spikes through winter into late spring. The fruits have a lemon-like taste.

Staghorn sumac *(Rhus typhina)*

**HOW TO GROW:** Plant sumac in a corner of your property or as a screen from neighbors, allowing plenty of room for this dramatic plant. It does well on steep slopes where it finds adequate drainage. In the fall, sumac leaves turn a dramatic flame red and the torch-like fruit spikes persist throughout the winter.

**BIRDS ATTRACTED:** At least 31 species are known to eat the fruit of this and other sumacs. Sumacs have value mainly as a late winter food for American Robin, Eastern Bluebird, Cedar Waxwing, Hermit Thrush, Northern Flicker, and Pileated Woodpecker. Sumacs offer little cover or nesting benefits.

**ALTERNATIVES:**

Smooth sumac *(Rhus glabra)* has a wide natural range from Maine to Florida and west to California and is hardier (to Zone 2) than staghorn sumac. Winged sumac *(R. copallina)* also develops spectacular color in the fall and has red spikes of fruit, but is a smaller shrub growing only 4' to 10'. Fragrant sumac *(R. aromatica)* is also a low shrub (4' to 8') that is drought-resistant, and prefers full sun and lime-stone soils.

## *Sambucus canadensis*
### AMERICAN ELDERBERRY

Many birds are attracted to the sweet, blue-black berries and use this dense, spreading shrub for cover and nesting. It grows 6' to 12' tall with an equal spread.

**NATIVE HABITAT:** In moist soil near ponds, streams, and wetlands.

**USDA HARDINESS ZONES:** 4 to 7

**FLOWERS AND FRUIT:** Flowers are creamy white and fragrant, forming broad, flat clusters that are 5" to 8" in diameter, appearing from June to August; fruits are small, juicy berries, ripening from July to September.

**HOW TO GROW:** Plant American elder-berry in moist soils near pond borders, springs, or stream beds. Use either sin-gle plants or plant in a cluster of three where space permits, to create a dense thicket habitat. Individual canes usually die back between the third and fifth year and should be removed. New plants are easily propagated by taking fall cuttings and keeping them in moist peat moss at 40° F through the winter. Then in the spring, plant them outside

in sunny locations.

**BIRDS ATTRACTED:** At least 37 species, including American Robin, Eastern Blue-bird, and Northern Mockingbird, feed on the sweet fruits, and nearly as many use the dense shrubs for cover. Several birds, including Alder Flycatcher, Gray Catbird, Yellow Warbler, and American Goldfinch, use elderberry for nesting.

**ALTERNATIVES:** Red elderberry (*Sambu-cus pubens*) has a similar growth habit and also requires wet soils. It has large clusters of bright red berries, and its wildlife values are similar to those of American elderberry.

## *Tsuga canadensis*
### EASTERN HEMLOCK

Eastern hemlock is an ideal plant for the bird gardener because of its tolerance for shade. It attracts many species, as it provides cover and nesting sites, and its seeds feed several species in winter. When young, it develops a graceful, spreading form up to 80', or a dense, compact form if pruned or sheared.

**NATIVE HABITAT:** Rocky ridges and ravines and cool, north-facing mountain slopes.

**USDA HARDINESS ZONES:** 3 to 7

**FLOWERS AND FRUIT:** Male and female cones appear September to October separately on the same plant and per-sist through the winter; seeds are in small, flexible cones. Trees growing in the open produce crops when they are

A Black-capped Chickadee eats seeds of eastern hemlock (*Tsuga canadensis*).

about 20 years old and have heavy crops every two to three years.

**HOW TO GROW:** Easily transplanted when given ample soil and grows well as a background landscape plant. When planted about 3' apart and sheared, plants form a dense hedge. Hemlock does poorly in hot, dry places. In some parts of the Northeast, woolly adelgid and aphids are serious pests. Check with your local nursery or Cooperative Extension agent before planting.

**BIRDS ATTRACTED:** Hemlock seeds are a preferred winter food for Carolina and Black-capped Chickadee, American Goldfinch, Red- and White-winged Crossbill, and Pine Siskin. Hemlock provides excellent cover in storms and night roosting for at least 22 species and nesting places for Mourning Dove, American Robin, Northern Cardinal, Wood Thrush, and many kinds of forest warblers.

**ALTERNATIVES:** White spruce *(Picea glauca)* provides nesting and winter cover for at least 19 species. It prefers more sun than hemlock and grows in either moist or well-drained soil.

*Viburnum recognitum*
**NORTHERN ARROWWOOD**
*Viburnum dentatum*
**SOUTHERN ARROWWOOD**
These very similar shrubs are erect (to 15'), and dense with a compact shape, especially when planted in full sun; they will also grow in partial shade. At least 26 species are known to eat viburnum fruit.

**NATIVE HABITAT:** Moist, low ground along streams and thickets.

**USDA HARDINESS ZONES:** Northern arrowwood, 2 to 7; southern arrowwood, 5 to 8

**FLOWERS AND FRUIT:** Flowers appear from June to August in white clusters 2" to 3" in diameter; fruits are small, oval, dark blue or black drupes in clusters that ripen from late August to November. The leaves in autumn turn dark bronze and deep red. The two species look very similar except that northern arrowwood has hairless twigs.

**HOW TO GROW:**

Plant arrowwoods where a dense border is desired. Plant in clumps of three along with other viburnums (see below), shrubby dogwoods, serviceberries, and other shrubs that favor edges. Both arrowwoods grow well in good soils. Their growth rate is moderate and they require little care after they are established. Deer usually avoid browsing on them.

Northern arrowwood

**BIRDS ATTRACTED:** Among the birds that eat arrowwood fruit are Eastern Phoebe, Brown Thrasher, Northern Flicker, White-eyed Vireo, Eastern Bluebird, and Rose-breasted Grosbeak. Gray Catbird uses arrowwood for cover and nesting.

**ALTERNATIVES:** American cranberrybush *(Viburnum opulus* var. *americanum)* holds its bright red fruits through the winter, providing food for early spring migrants; nannyberry *(Viburnum lentago)* is a large shrub, growing to 10' to 20' tall; it has brilliant red-purple fall foliage and blue-black fruits that dry on the shrub, giving it its alternate name, wild raisin. It is hardy to Zone 2 and grows rapidly.

## MORE GREAT BIRD PLANTS FOR THE NORTHEAST

*Trees*
Black Cherry *(Prunus serotina)*
zones 4 to 8
Blackgum *(Nyssa sylvatica)* zones 5 to 9
Cockspur Hawthorn *(Crataegus
crus-galli)* zones 5 to 9
Common Hackberry *(Celtis
occidentalis)* zones 2 to 9
Crabapples *(Malus* species)
zones 5 to 8
Eastern Red Cedar *(Juniperus
viginiana)* zones 3 to 9
Mountain Ash *(Sorbus americana)*
zones 3 to 8
Pagoda (Alternate-leaved) Dogwood
*(Cornus alternifolia)* zones 4 to 8
Red Mulberry *(Morus rubra)*
zones 6 to 9
Sweet Black Birch *(Betula lenta)*
zones 4 to 7
Washington Hawthorn *(Crataegus
phaenopyrum)* zones 4 to 8
White Oak *(Quercus alba)* zones 5 to 8

*Shrubs*
Black Huckleberry *(Gaylussacia
baccata)* zones 2 to 8
Blackberries and raspberries *(Rubus
species)* zones 3 to 7
Coralberry *(Symphoricarpos
orbiculatus)* zones 2 to 8

Highbush Blueberry *(Vaccinium
corymbosum)* zones 4 to 8
Lowbush Blueberry *(V. angustifolium)*
zones 2 to 6
Northern Bayberry *(Myrica
pennsylvanica)* zones 2 to 6

*Groundcovers and Vines*
Bearberry *(Arctostaphylos uva-ursi)*
zones 2 to 6
Creeping Juniper *(Juniperus
horizontalis)* zones 4 to 6
Partridgeberry *(Mitchella repens)*
zones 2 to 6
Strawberry *(Fragaria virginiana)*
zones 4 to 8
Trumpet Creeper *(Campsis radicans)*
zones 5 to 8

SOUTHEAST

# The Southeast

BY DANIEL M. SAVERCOOL

*Callicarpa americana*

**BEAUTYBERRY**

Beautyberry produces a profusion of brilliantly colored fruits that persist on the plants from early fall to late winter; these are favored by a number of birds.

**NATIVE HABITAT:** Flatwoods, scrub, live oak and maritime hummocks, fence-rows, mixed hardwoods, and shrub thickets.

**USDA HARDINESS ZONES:** 7 to 10

**FLOWERS AND FRUIT:** Beautyberry has white to pink flowers, which it produces in axillary clusters at the base of the leaves. The fruits—round, purple to magenta drupes, about ¼" in diameter—are produced in clusters in late summer to early fall, and persist until spring.

**HOW TO GROW:** Plant beautyberry after all threat of frost has passed until about three months before the first frost, in acid soil containing moderate to high levels of organic matter. You can propagate plants from seed, cuttings, and layering, or buy nursery-grown specimens in a range of sizes. Beautyberry tolerates partial shade to full sun.

Woodpeckers and Northern Cardinal are attracted to the fruit of beautyberry.

BIRDS ATTRACTED: Several southeastern birds eat the fruits of the beautyberry, including Bobwhite Quail, woodpeckers, Northern Cardinal, American Robin, Northern Mockingbird, and Brown Thrasher.

ALTERNATIVES: Among the more than 40 species of *Callicarpa* worldwide, only *C. americana* is native to the U.S. However, other species in the verbena family (Verbenaceae) that may be alternatives are fiddlewood *(Citharexylum fruticosum)* and golden dewdrop *(Duranta repens)*. These all produce fruits similar in wildlife value to those of beautyberry.

*Helianthus debilis*
## BEACH SUNFLOWER
This annual herb can grow to 4' in length but seldom exceeds a height of 12". In late summer and early fall, beach sunflower produces a multitude of seeds that are eaten by seed-eating birds.

NATIVE HABITAT: Coastal beaches and other dry areas in full sun.

USDA HARDINESS ZONES: 7 to 10

FLOWERS AND FRUIT: Flowers are bright yellow with a reddish purple corolla, and are about 2" in diameter. Beach sunflower will flower year-round if planted in full sun. It produces clusters of soft-walled seeds (achenes) in summer.

HOW TO GROW: Plant beach sunflower after the last frost and until three months before the first frost in a neutral to somewhat alkaline, well-drained soil that contains little organic matter. Plants will not thrive if they are continually damp, but in other respects are very hardy, requiring little attention.

BIRDS ATTRACTED: American Goldfinch and Eastern Meadowlark are likely to eat the seeds of the beach sunflower, and the seeds of other sunflowers are enthusiastically eaten by many songbirds.

ALTERNATIVES: More than 20 species of *Helianthus* are native to the Southeast. The narrow-leaved sunflower *(H. angustifolius)* is a good alternative, with an appearance and seeds that are simlar to beach sunflower.

Beach sunflower (*Helianthus debilis*)

SOUTHEAST

**SOUTHEAST**

*Ilex cassine*

**DAHOON HOLLY**

This species, along with other native hollies, is an important part of the winter landscape. Hollies are one of the few plants that produce berries late in fall, providing food for birds when other sources have disappeared and nutrition is crucial.

NATIVE HABITAT: Wet soils in forested habitats (cypress ponds, swamps, hummocks, and bayheads), depressions, marshes, and stream banks.

USDA HARDINESS ZONES: 7 to 10

FLOWERS AND FRUIT: Dahoon holly plants are either male or female and both plants are needed for fruit production; however, because the plant is common, it is not imperative to have both in the landscape. On both male and female plants, the flowers are white and about ¼" across; on the male, the flowers appear in clusters, while those of the female plants are borne singly or in groups of two to three. Female plants produce bunches of bright red to orange fruits, each about ¼" in diameter, in late summer to early fall; these persist until spring.

HOW TO GROW: For best results, plant dahoon holly after the threat of frost is past until about three months before the first frost. Dahoon holly can be relatively difficult to propagate, but you can try growing it from seed or by placing cuttings under glass. Plant in the garden in rich, slightly acid soil; dahoon holly likes moist conditions, so be sure to plant where the soil is continually moist.

BIRDS ATTRACTED: At least 26 bird species feed on the fruits of the dahoon holly, including Wild Turkey, Eastern Bluebird, Gray Catbird, Northern Mockingbird, American Robin, and Brown Thrasher.

ALTERNATIVES: Several holly species are native to the Southeast, including American holly *(I. opaca)*, yaupon holly *(I. vomitoria)*, sweet gallberry *(I. coriacea)*, and myrtle-leaved holly *(I. myrtifolia)*. All produce fruits in the late fall, providing food for birds over the winter.

*Ilex vomitoria*

**YAUPON HOLLY**

As with the fruits of many hollies, those of this tall, evergreen shrub are favored by a number of bird species. They also find abundant nesting sites in its branches.

NATIVE HABITAT: Dunes to maritime woods, pond margins, swamps, sparse woods, and fencerows.

USDA HARDINESS ZONES: 7 to 9

FLOWERS AND FRUIT: Flowers are small, white, and unisexual (male and female flowers occur on separate trees). Male plants produce flowers in clusters, while the flowers of the female plant are borne singly or in groups of two to

Many birds eat the fruit of yaupon holly (*Ilex vomitoria*) during fall and winter.

three. In late summer to early fall, plants produce dense clusters of bright red to crimson fruits, about ¼" in diameter, that persist on branches until spring.

**HOW TO GROW:** Plant yaupon holly in full sun when there is no threat of frost, in rich, slightly acid soil. This species can grow to 45' and takes particularly well to trimming; in fact, it is one of the shrubs commonly used to create topiaries.

**BIRDS ATTRACTED:** Approximately 26 birds are known to eat yaupon holly fruit throughout the late fall and winter, including Wild Turkey, Eastern Bluebird, Gray Catbird, Northern Mockingbird, American Robin, and Brown Thrasher.

**ALTERNATIVES:** Several species of holly are native to the Southeast, including American holly *(I. opaca)*, dahoon holly *(I. cassine)*, sweet gallberry *(I. coriacea)*, and myrtle-leaved holly *(I. myrtifolia)*, and all are favored by birds.

---

*Juniperus silicicola*
**SOUTHERN RED CEDAR**
This evergreen, coniferous tree provides fruits, nesting sites, and shelter to a number of bird species.

**NATIVE HABITAT:** Thin woods or open habitats along coastal areas, from established dunes and brackish sites to the edges of successional forests.

**USDA HARDINESS ZONES:** 7 to 10

**FLOWERS AND FRUIT:** Male and female cones are produced in winter on sepa-

Coral honeysuckle

as excellent nesting habitat.

**ALTERNATIVES:** The southern red cedar is closely related to the eastern red cedar *(J. virginiana);* the former is found in coastal settings, while the latter grows inland. The two are most easily distinguished by their shapes; both are cone-shaped, but the southern red cedar has a rounded top, while the eastern has a pointed top. They have similar wildlife value.

rate trees; male cones are approximately 2" long; the female cones are much smaller, to ¼" long, and are bluish and berry-like.

**HOW TO GROW:** Plant in neutral, well-drained soil in full sun to full shade. Do not plant cedars near hawthorn or apple (including crabapple) trees, as the southern red cedar is a host for apple rust.

**BIRDS ATTRACTED:** Several species of birds eat the cones of this plant, including Cedar Waxwing, Eastern Bluebird, Tree Swallow, Yellow-rumped Warbler, Northern Flicker, Yellow-bellied Sapsucker, American Robin, and Northern Mockingbird. An evergreen, this tree provides shelter during storms as well

*Lonicera sempervirens*
### CORAL HONEYSUCKLE

Coral honeysuckle's juicy berries are favored by several bird species, and hummingbirds sip its nectar.

**NATIVE HABITAT:** Thin woods, fencerows, and shrub thickets.

**USDA HARDINESS ZONES:** 7 to 10

**FLOWERS AND FRUIT:** Flowers are orange-scarlet and yellow inside, 2" long, and in terminal clusters. The fruits—round, red, juicy berries about 1/4" in diameter—are produced in terminal clusters in summer.

**HOW TO GROW:** Plant in acid soils containing moderate to high levels of organic matter, in partial shade to full sun. Provide a support structure for this vining plant or use it as a groundcover. You can also train it to grow as a neat, climbing vertical shrub. Except in southern Florida, where it is evergreen, this vine is deciduous.

Southern magnolia produces fragrant flowers and red berries for the birds.

**SOUTHEAST**

**BIRDS ATTRACTED:** Several birds eat the fruit, including Bobwhite Quail, Wild Turkey, Purple Finch, American Goldfinch, and American Robin. Ruby-throated Hummingbird feeds on the nectar.

**ALTERNATIVES:** There are numerous species of *Lonicera* found throughout the United States. The following varieties and cultivars are similar in their wildlife value to the species: *Lonicera sempervirens* var. *minor*, 'Magnifica', 'Sulphurea', and 'Superba'. Several bird species forage for the fruit of Japanese honeysuckle, but it is invasive and should not be planted.

*Magnolia grandiflora*
## SOUTHERN MAGNOLIA
Southern magnolia often grows among live oaks and bay trees. Its fruits and foliage provide food and shelter for a multitude of songbirds.

**NATIVE HABITAT:** Upland forests, coastal hummocks, and swamp margins.

**USDA HARDINESS ZONES:** 7 to 10

**FLOWERS AND FRUIT:** Southern magnolia produces flowers throughout the summer that are large (6" to 8" in diameter), creamy white, and very fragrant. The fruit, cone-like in shape and up to 6", is covered with bright red berries.

**HOW TO GROW:** Specimens may be purchased small as liners or balled and burlapped, or as several sizes of potted material. Plant trees after the threat of frost to about three months before the first frost, to allow the tree to overcome transplant shock before winter. Southern magnolia can be propagated from seed sown in the fall, by grafting, and by soft cuttings under glass. Plant in rich, somewhat moist, and slightly acid soils.

**BIRDS ATTRACTED:** A number of songbird species, such as Red-eyed Vireo, towhees, and Red-cockaded Woodpecker, eat the berries of the southern magnolia, and many birds find shelter in the evergreen foliage.

**ALTERNATIVES:** Several other species in the magnolia family are native to this region, but only the sweetbay magnolia *(M. virginiana)* can be found easily in nurseries and produces a fruit that birds will readily eat.

*Muhlenbergia capillaris*
## PURPLE MUHLY GRASS
Songbirds forage for seeds in clumps of this grass and find its dead blades useful as nest material.

**NATIVE HABITAT:** Sandhills, flatwoods, bogs, coastal swales, and wet prairies.

**USDA HARDINESS ZONES:** 5 to 10

**FLOWERS AND FRUIT:** This grass produces a pink to purple inflorescence about half as long as the entire plant. When the panicles are in full color in late summer to early fall they are very attractive, especially if planted in clumps.

**HOW TO GROW:** Plant in soil containing low to medium amounts of organic matter that is neutral to slightly acid and

Purple muhly grass

Brown Thrasher is one of many birds that eats the fruits of wax myrtle.

moderately to poorly drained. Purple muhly grass prefers partial shade to open, sunny spots.

**BIRDS ATTRACTED:** Many seed-eating songbirds, such as sparrows.

**ALTERNATIVES:** Nimbleweed *(M. schreberi)* and other clumping species among the grass family (Poaceae) provide similar benefits to birds.

---

*Myrica cerifera*
### WAX MYRTLE

This evergreen shrub, to 35', will flourish in a wide range of soil conditions. It provides not only fruits to many bird species, but also shelter and nesting sites.

**NATIVE HABITAT:** Forest edges between mature forests and grassy meadows.

**USDA HARDINESS ZONES:** 6 to 10

**HOW TO GROW:** Wax myrtle is highly adaptable, thriving in partial to full sun, in a range of soils—high to low organic content, variable pH, well or poorly drained.

**FLOWERS AND FRUIT:** Flowers, catkins about 1" long, are produced in profusion in spring. In late summer to early fall, female plants produce fruits— waxy, bluish drupes less than ¼" in diameter. Both male and female plants are needed to produce fruits, but as they are common in the region, it is not necessary to have both in the landscape.

**BIRDS ATTRACTED:** More than 25 species of birds eat wax myrtle fruit, including

Florida Duck, King Rail, Wild Turkey, Eastern Bluebird, Yellow-rumped Warbler, White-eyed Vireo, Ruby-crowned Kinglet, Tree Swallow, Bobwhite Quail, Carolina Chickadee, Eastern Meadowlark, Tree Swallow, Tufted Titmouse, and Red-cockaded Woodpecker. An evergreen, this shrub provides shelter and nesting sites to many species.
**ALTERNATIVES:** Six species of *Myrica* are native to the eastern U.S. Other species common to the Southeast include the odorless bayberry *(M. inodora)* and swamp candleberry *(M. heterophylla)*.

Live oak (*Quercus virginiana*)

---

## *Quercus virginiana*
### LIVE OAK

Live oak is the dominant species in oak hummocks throughout the Southeast, and its acorns are favored by more than 15 bird species.
**NATIVE HABITAT:** Dry, sandy soils in relatively low-elevation habitats, such as the bases of sand dunes and around depressional wetlands.
**USDA HARDINESS ZONES:** 7 to 10
**FLOWERS AND FRUIT:** Male flowers are hanging catkins 1" to 1¼" long. The fruit is a dark brown, shiny acorn, oblong in shape, and approximately ¾" long.
**HOW TO GROW:**
Plant this deciduous tree with a spreading canopy of up to 60 feet in neutral, well-drained soil, after the last frost has passed.
**BIRDS ATTRACTED:** More than 15 species consume the acorn of the live oak, including Wood Duck, Bobwhite Quail, Florida Scrub Jay, Eastern Meadowlark, Brown Thrasher, Red-headed Woodpecker, Blue Jay, and Red-cockaded Woodpecker.
**ALTERNATIVES:** Approximately 23 other oak species are native to the Southeast, in habitats ranging from dry scrub to forested wetland. These species will produce acorns in numbers comparable to live oak: Chapman oak *(Q. chapmanii)*, southern red oak *(Q. falcata)*, sand live oak *(Q. geminata)*, laurel oak *(Q. hemisphaerica)*, and turkey oak *(Q. laevis)*.

*Serenoa repens*

**SAW PALMETTO**

Not only does this hardy native have attractive, fan-shaped leaves up to 3' across, but its fruits are favored by several bird species.

**NATIVE HABITAT:**

Diverse habitats from inland scrub communities to swamp and marsh edges, and from mesic hardwood hummocks to coastal dunes.

**USDA HARDINESS ZONES:** 7 to 10

**FLOWERS AND FRUIT:** Flowers are greenish white, borne in spiky clusters from among the leaves. Fruits, produced in late summer to early fall, are oblong drupes, black when mature, about ½" in diameter, and in clusters. They persist until spring.

**HOW TO GROW:** This upright, evergreen shrubby palm can grow to 20' tall, but it can also grow into a low prostrate form to 6'. Saw palmetto can survive in very dry conditions, preferring sandy soils and lots of sun, but cannot tolerate even short periods of wetness. Soil type can vary in organic content, but should be low in pH and moderately to well drained.

**BIRDS ATTRACTED:** Six bird species feed on the fruits of the saw palmetto, including Fish Crow, Northern Mockingbird, American Robin, Myrtle Warbler, and Pileated and Red-bellied Woodpecker.

**ALTERNATIVES:** Viable alternatives in the palm family (Palmae) include the nee-

dle palm *(Rhapidophyllum hystrix)*, scrub palmetto *(Sabal etonia)*, and dwarf palmetto *(Sabal minor)*.

*Viburnum obovatum*

**WALTER'S VIBURNUM**

This shrub is most important to birds as refuge and nesting habitat, but its fruits also feed several species.

**NATIVE HABITAT:** Moist soils along stream banks and flood plains and in hammocks; occasionally found in dry uplands in areas underlain with limestone.

**USDA HARDINESS ZONES:** 8 to 9

**FLOWERS AND FRUIT:** Small white flowers appear in clusters (to 6" in diameter) in late winter to early spring. The fruit, produced in late summer to early fall, is a black drupe, up to ¼" in diameter.

**HOW TO GROW:** Walter's viburnum prefers partial sun, and will flower more profusely as it gets more sun. This species often produces suckers from its shallow roots, which you can transplant elsewhere. Plant in rich, acid soil that drains poorly to moderately well.

**BIRDS ATTRACTED:** While the number of birds that forage in this species is limited (including Wild Turkey, Northern Cardinal, American Robin, Brown Thrasher, and Pileated Woodpecker), its dense twig network and persistent leaves provide excellent refuge and

**SOUTHEAST**

nesting habitat for many bird species, including Northern Mockingbird.
**ALTERNATIVES:** Rusty blackhaw *(V. rufidulum)*, blackhaw *(V. prunifolium)*, swamphaw *(V. cassinoides)*, and possumhaw viburnum (*V. nudum*) are other viburnums common to the Southeast that are favored by birds.

## MORE GREAT BIRD PLANTS FOR THE SOUTHEAST

*Trees*
American Holly *(Ilex opaca)*
    zones 5 to 9
Blackgum *(Nyssa sylvatica)* zones 5 to 9
Hickories *(Carya* species) zones 5 to 9
Longleaf Pine *(Pinus palustris)*
    zones 7 to 9
Red Maple *(Acer rubrum)* zones 5 to 10
River Birch *(Betula nigra)* zones 7 to 9
Sassafras *(Sassafras albidum)*
    zones 5 to 9
Sugarberry *(Celtis laevigata)*
    zones 6 to 9
Sweetgum *(Liquidambar styraciflua)*
    zones 6 to 9

*Shrubs*
Blueberries *(Vaccinium* species)
    zones 7 to 10
Buttonbush *(Cephalanthus occidentalis)*
    zones 4 to 9

Chickasaw Plum *(Prunus angustifolia)*
    zones 7 to 9
Coastal Plain Willow *(Salix caroliniana)*
    zones 6 to 10
Flowering Dogwood *(Cornus florida)*;
    Stiff Cornel *(C. foemina)* zones 5 to 9
Gallberry, Inkberry *(Ilex glabra)*
    zones 5 to 10
Redbud *(Cercis canadensis)*
    zones 6 to 9
Red Mulberry *(Morus rubra)*
    zones 5 to 9
Swamp Rose *(Rosa palustris)*
    zones 5 to 9

*Groundcovers, Vines, and Grasses*
Blazing Stars *(Liatris* species)
    zones 5 to 9
Butterfly Weed *(Asclepias tuberosa)*
    zones 5 to 10
Cardinal Flower *(Lobelia cardinalis)*
    zones 5 to 9
Carolina Jessamine *(Gelsemium sempervirens)* zones 7 to 9
Coontie *(Zamia pumila)* zone 9
Gama Grass *(Tripsacum dactyloides)*
    zones 6 to 9
Indian Blanketflower *(Gaillardia pulchella)* zones 7 to 9
Sand Cordgrass *(Spartina bakeri)*
    zones 8 to 10
Trumpet Creeper *(Campsis radicans)*
    zones 6 to 10
Virginia Creeper *(Parthenocissus quinquefolia)* zones 5 to 9

The Northern Flicker nests in tree cavities and eats insects, fruit, and nuts.

SOUTHEAST

# South Florida

## BY DANIEL M. SAVERCOOL

Unfortunately, because southern Florida occupies such a small portion of the continent and has such a specialized climate, few studies have been conducted of the behavior of birds of the region, and those that have been done elsewhere aren't applicable to this tropical climate and its native species. As you'll see below, there is little information about how birds use the common native plants of southern Florida. In South Florida, sunlight is the limiting factor in plant growth, while in all other areas of the continent, plants' ability to survive freezing temperatures is the limiting factor. The birds found in South Florida and the Florida Keys are either transients that are on their way to breeding or wintering grounds elsewhere, or are residents that are on the outskirts of their range. As you think about designing your bird-friendly landscape in South Florida, don't be dismayed at the dearth of information about how birds use the native plants. In lieu of this information, learn to rely on your own judgment and follow these simple rules: if a plant's fruit looks attractive to birds—if it is fleshy and brightly colored—and if the plant has evergreen leaves or dense branches that birds could use as refuge, and the plant is native to the area, give it a try. Chances are that birds will like it. And if it looks nice and the birds use it, you will like it, too.

*Acoelorraphe wrightii*
**PAUROTIS PALM**
The paurotis is a very popular landscaping palm that forms impressively large clumps in the landscape.
**NATIVE HABITAT:** Edges of hardwood hammocks and open areas of the Everglades region of South Florida and the Caribbean.
**USDA HARDINESS ZONE:** 12
**FLOWERS AND FRUIT:** Paurotis palm bears yellow-green flowers on long stalks from the base of the leaves. Its fruits, which form in summer, are globular drupes about ½" long and black when mature.
**HOW TO GROW:** Paurotis palm is available in nurseries or can be propagated from seed or by dividing the rootball. Plant in soil that contains high levels of both organic matter and sand, has a neutral pH and medium moisture–holding capacity, and is relatively well drained.
**BIRDS ATTRACTED:** The wildlife value of the paurotis palm has not been studied

Paurotis palm attracts birds in summer with its black berries.

well, but because of the size and shape of its fruits, it's likely that several fruit- and berry-eating tropical and subtropical birds consume them. These include the White-crowned Pigeon, Pileated Woodpecker, Fish Crow, and Northern Mockingbird.

**ALTERNATIVES:** This is the only species of *Acoelorraphe* native to South Florida, but other species in the palm family, such as Key thatch palm *(Thrinax morrisii)*, silver palm *(Coccothrinax argentata)*, and Florida thatch palm *(Thrinax radiata)*, are good alternatives, as their structures and fruit are similar to those of paurotis palm.

Sea ox-eye daisy *(Borrichia frutescens)*

## *Borrichia frutescens*
### SEA OX-EYE DAISY

Sea ox-eye daisy is a stiff-branching, upright shrub to 4' tall.

**NATIVE HABITAT:** Margins and higher elevations of salt and brackish marshes.

**USDA HARDINESS ZONES:** 7 to 10

**FLOWERS AND FRUIT:** Each plant produces a profusion of yellow flowers, about 1½" in diameter, throughout the year. Fruits are a soft-walled seed (achene) approximately ¼" long produced from summer to fall.

**HOW TO GROW:** In the wild, the sea ox-eye daisy commonly grows in estuarine wetlands, but it can survive in a variety of soils—high to low in organic content, with acid to alkaline pH, moderately to poorly drained—as long as the soil is kept moist. In cooler parts of the region, this species is an annual.

**BIRDS ATTRACTED:** Naturalists do not have much information on the wildlife use of this species, but they suspect that seed-eating birds are attracted to the achenes, and butterflies have been observed feeding on flower nectar.

**ALTERNATIVES:** Other members of the sunflower family (Asteraceae) that are viable alternatives include the marsh elder *(Iva frutescens)* and the seashore elder *(I. imbricata)*. The sea ox-eye *B. arborescens* is similar to *B. frutescens* in range, but the former grows taller and has more of a tree-like form.

*Bursera simaruba*

## GUMBO LIMBO

Gumbo limbo is a medium-sized, spreading tree that can grow as tall as 60'. It has another common name—the tourist tree—which derives from its red and peeling bark.

NATIVE HABITAT: Coastal and tropical hammocks.

USDA HARDINESS ZONES: 9 to 10

FLOWERS AND FRUIT: Small white flowers up to 5" long are produced in spring in clusters. Although the flowers last only one day, they begin producing nectar before dawn, so at daybreak the flowers are the site of intense bee activity. The fruit, a small (½" long) drupe, is produced in fall and winter.

HOW TO GROW: Gumbo limbo is very tolerant of salt, drought, and poor soil; it will grow best, though, in a well drained soil that contains a moderate level of organic matter mixed with sand and a neutral to slightly alkaline pH. Gumbo limbo can be propagated from seed or by cuttings of green wood.

BIRDS ATTRACTED:

Many of the seed-eating birds of South Florida, such as Northern Mockingbird, vireos, warblers, and flycatchers, forage on the fruits of this species. The hard seeds are also believed to serve the function of pebbles in a bird's giz-

SOUTH FLORIDA

Birds are attracted to the seeds of gumbo limbo, while bees like its nectar.

zard, the muscular structure that birds use to grind hard seeds before digesting them.

ALTERNATIVES: Gumbo limbo is the only representative of the Torchwood family (Burseraceae) that is native to South Florida.

Cocoplum (*Chrysobalanus icaco*)

---

*Chrysobalanus icaco*
## COCOPLUM
This evergreen shrub or small bushy tree grows to 15' tall.

NATIVE HABITAT: Low hummocks, cypress heads, beaches, sand dunes, and other wet coastal habitats, and occasionally inland swamps and disturbed transitional zones between wetlands and uplands.

USDA HARDINESS ZONES: 9 to 10

FLOWERS AND FRUIT: Flowers are small, white, bell-shaped, and produced in clusters throughout the year. Fruits are round, purple to yellowish drupes, about ¾" to 1" in diameter.

HOW TO GROW: Cocoplum can be propagated from seed, if the seed is cracked before planting, from hardwood cuttings, and by layering. Plant in moderately to poorly drained soil with medium to high levels of organic matter and a neutral to alkaline pH.

BIRDS ATTRACTED: While little quantitative data currently link the cocoplum to bird foraging, the flesh of the fruit is high in sugar and the kernel is high in fat, so the fruit is likely to be an excellent source of energy for birds. The nectar is used by bees for honey production.

ALTERNATIVES: With the exception of gopher apple *(Licania michauxii)*, which grows in scrub communities and is approximately 6" tall, cocoplum is the only species of the cocoplum family (Chrysobalanaceae) native to the U.S.

---

*Coccoloba diversifolia*
## PIGEON PLUM
The evergreen pigeon plum is a common street tree in southern Florida and the Caribbean, to 60' tall.

NATIVE HABITAT: Hardwood hammocks and willow sloughs.

USDA HARDINESS ZONE: 10

**FLOWERS AND FRUIT:** Flowers are whitish green and about ¼" across, borne in long racemes (stalked flowers arranged along an axis and opening from the bottom up) and unisexual, with the sexes on separate trees. The flowers are produced in spring. Fruits are dark red, about ⅓" in diameter, and oblong in shape. The fruits are produced in late summer to early fall.

**HOW TO GROW:** Pigeon plum is commonly planted in South Florida along city streets; it's very hardy, and thrives in the full sun and high temperatures of South Florida's urban areas. Plant in a well-drained but moisture-retentive, acid soil containing high levels of both organic matter and sand. Pigeon plum can be propagated from seed, by transplanting the suckers, by layering, or by placing cuttings under glass.

**BIRDS ATTRACTED:** Naturalists believe that the edible but bitter fruit is eaten by several fruit- and berry-eating tropical and subtropical birds, including the White-crowned Pigeon, Pileated Woodpecker, Fish Crow, and Northern Mockingbird.

**ALTERNATIVES:** Several species of *Coccoloba* are found in the tropical U.S. and Caribbean. Its close relative the sea grape *(C. uvifera*, below) is perhaps the most readily available viable alternative.

Pigeon plum (*Coccoloba diversifolia*)

## *Coccoloba uvifera*
### SEA GRAPE

Sea grape, an evergreen, can vary in habit from a low, spreading shrub to a small tree, to 25' tall.

**NATIVE HABITAT:** Coastal scrub.

**USDA HARDINESS ZONE:** 10

**FLOWERS AND FRUIT:** Very small, greenish flowers are produced at the ends of long stems throughout the year. The 1"-long fruits are egg-shaped and produced in grape-like clusters; they are purple when mature. Unlike the fruit of the pigeon plum *(C. diversifolia)*, that of the sea grape is sweet.

**HOW TO GROW:** Sea grape is commonly planted along roadsides and parking

SOUTH FLORIDA

lots because of its ability to endure dry conditions and full sun. Plant in a well-drained, neutral soil that contains moderate levels of organic matter and sand. Sea grape can be propagated from seed, by layering, or by placing cuttings of mature wood under glass.

**BIRDS ATTRACTED:** Little quantitative data exist of the wildlife value of the sea grape, but it is likely that the fruit is eaten by several of the larger fruit- and berry-eating tropical and subtropical birds, including the White-crowned Pigeon, Pileated Woodpecker, Fish Crow, and Northern Mockingbird.

**ALTERNATIVES:** Several species of *Coccoloba* are found in the tropical U.S. and Caribbean. Its close relative the pigeon

Coral bean (*Erythrina herbacea*)

plum *(C. diversifolia)* is perhaps the most readily available viable alternative. Sea grape has a much larger leaf than pigeon plum.

---

## *Erythrina herbacea*
## CORAL BEAN

Coral bean can vary from a shrub, to a small tree, to 20'.

**NATIVE HABITAT:** Low-elevation dry forests.

**USDA HARDINESS ZONES:** 7 to 10

**FLOWERS AND FRUIT:** Flowers are bright red, to 2-1/2" long, and tubular, borne in vertical racemes. The flowers are produced in late spring to early summer. The fruit of the coral bean is produced in a 4"- to 6"-long pod, which splits open in fall revealing a hard, scarlet seed. The seeds are somewhat toxic to humans and have been used as a fish poison.

**HOW TO GROW:** Deciduous coral bean is salt-tolerant, prefers full sun to partial shade, and well-drained, dry soil with moderate levels of organics mixed with sand, and a neutral to slightly alkaline pH. Coral bean can be propagated from seed but only if first scarified—abraded so that the seed coat begins to break down—or by cuttings of growing wood.

**BIRDS ATTRACTED:** The tubular red flowers are very attractive to hummingbirds.

**ALTERNATIVES:** There are more than 15

other species of *Erythrina* located in the Caribbean and Central and South America. *E. herbacea* var. *arborea* is also found in the Southeast U.S. and South Florida and is a draw for hummingbirds.

## *Ipomoea pes-caprae*
### RAILROAD VINE

Railroad vine gets its name from its long and straight growing habit. This trailing, fleshy perennial will grow to more than 60' long and 1' tall.

Railroad vine (*Ipomoea pes-caprae*)

**NATIVE HABITAT:** Subtropical to tropical coasts along the high tide line of beaches, on dunes, and on overwash flats.

**USDA HARDINESS ZONES:** 7 to 10

**FLOWERS AND FRUIT:** This morning glory produces large (2" in diameter) bluish to purple flowers throughout the year. When the fruit capsules mature, plants release orange seeds approximately ¼" in diameter.

**HOW TO GROW:** In the wild, railroad vine commonly grows in full sun. After a frost, its foliage will die back but a viable root system remains. This vine should be planted after the threat of frost to about three months prior to the first frost. Soil type can vary in organic content from low to medium, in pH from medium to alkaline, and in drainage from moderate to sharp. Railroad vine is commonly propagated from seed and stem and leaf cuttings.

**BIRDS ATTRACTED:** The railroad vine produces a showy flower and numerous seeds, suggesting that it would be a popular foraging plant for birds.

**ALTERNATIVES:** Several species of morning glory are native to this region, including the fiddle leaf morning glory *(I. imperati [I. stolonifera])* and the coastal morning glory *(I. cordatotriloba [I. trichocarpa])*.

## *Jacquinia keyensis*
### JOEWOOD

This evergreen shrub to small tree will grow as tall as 20'.

**NATIVE HABITAT:** Diverse habitats from coastal scrub to beach berms.

**USDA HARDINESS ZONE:** 10

**FLOWERS AND FRUIT:** Flowers are white to pale yellow clusters, approximately ¼" long, funnel-shaped, and fragrant, and are produced in late winter to spring. The fruits are round berries, yellow to orange-red, and about ½" in diameter. The fruits are produced in late summer to early fall and persist until spring.

**HOW TO GROW:** Joewood can grow in very dry conditions as well as where the roots are periodically inundated by wave action. It can be propagated from seed or by cuttings. Joewood is not fussy about soil drainage or organic content but prefers a neutral to alkaline pH.

**BIRDS ATTRACTED:** This species is used by birds for refuge and nesting in a wide range of habitats in the extreme southern tip of Florida and the Keys.

Joewood berries are toxic to fish and some insects, but are known to be eaten by birds and other wildlife.

**ALTERNATIVES:** The only other member of the theophrasta family (Theophrastaceae), torchwood (*J. arborea*) is native to the Caribbean islands, excluding the Bahamas. Torchwood is also found in the Florida Keys, most probably having naturalized there.

*Lycium carolinianum*
**CHRISTMAS BERRY**

Christmas berry, an evergreen shrub to small tree, will reach 10' tall.

**NATIVE HABITAT:** Coastal areas on sandy mounds and ridges in salt marshes, and

Christmas berry feeds birds that migrate to the Florida Keys in winter.

along brackish shores and ditches.

**USDA HARDINESS ZONES:** 8 to 10

**FLOWERS AND FRUIT:** Flowers are solitary, white to a bluish-lavender, ¼" long, and are produced in summer. The fruits are bright red, juicy berries to ½" in diameter, and are produced in late fall and winter.

**HOW TO GROW:** Christmas berry is adaptable to many soil types but prefers low organic matter mixed with sand, neutral to slightly alkaline pH, and poor drainage. It can be propagated from seed, by layering, by transplanting suckers, or by rooting cuttings of mature wood.

**BIRDS ATTRACTED:** This is a favorite food source of numerous birds, including

Simpson stopper (*Myrcianthes fragrans*)

winter migrants to the Keys region of South Florida, such as American Robin, White-crowned Pigeon, and Northern Mockingbird.

**ALTERNATIVES:** Other species in the nightshade family (Solanaceae) native to this region include the cankerberry *(Solanum bahamense)* and the potato tree *(S. erianthum)*.

---

*Myrcianthes fragrans*
**SIMPSON STOPPER**

This evergreen shrub to small tree will reach 30'.

**NATIVE HABITAT:** Sub-tropical hardwood hammocks.

**USDA HARDINESS ZONES:** 9 to 10

**FLOWERS AND FRUIT:** Small, white flowers appear in long, stalked clusters in spring. In the fall, plants produce fruits that are round, red drupes to ¼" in diameter.

**HOW TO GROW:** Simpson stopper prefers full to partial shade, moist soil, and high humidity. Plant in moderately drained, acid soil with a high organic content. Simpson stopper can be propagated from seed or from cuttings.

**BIRDS ATTRACTED:** Little quantitative data exists on how wildlife use this species, but it is likely that its fruits are eaten by bird species such as Blue Jay, Brown Thrasher, and Northern Mockingbird.

**ALTERNATIVES:** Six other species of stopper are native to South Florida, including Spanish stopper *(Eugenia foetida)*, white stopper *(E. axillaris)*, red stopper *(E. rhombea)*, redberry stopper *(E. confusa)* and long-stalked stopper *(Psidium longipes)*.

Sea oats *(Uniola paniculata)*

---

*Uniola paniculata*

## SEA OATS

The foliage of this perennial grass can grow to 3' and its seed heads can reach 6'.

**NATIVE HABITAT:** Dunes, beaches, and loose sands near shores.

**USDA HARDINESS ZONES:** 7 to 10

**HOW TO GROW:** Sea oats, one of the main species found in the coastal dune habitat, is very hardy and doesn't require much attention. Plant in a well-drained soil that has a low organic content and a neutral to alkaline pH; this species does not like to be damp. Sea oats is commonly propagated from seed and by division. Because this grass is so valuable for dune stabilization, it's illegal to collect the seeds in many states, but specimens are available in regional nurseries.

**FLOWERS AND FRUIT:** The flowering part of the grass, a long stem holding spikelets of seeds, is produced from summer to early fall.

**BIRDS ATTRACTED:** While little quantitative data exist on the wildlife use of this grass, seed-eating songbirds probably forage on the oats.

**ALTERNATIVES:** Spike grass *(Leptochloopsis virgata [Uniola virgata])*, a related species found in the Caribbean, or the inland dry habitat spangle grass *(Chasmanthium laxum var. sessiliflorum)*, which is native to the Southeast, are good alternatives.

## MORE GREAT BIRD PLANTS FOR SOUTH FLORIDA

*Trees*

Slash Pine *(Pinus elliotii* var. *densa)*
zones 9 to 10

Green Buttonwood *(Conocarpus erectus)* zones 9 to 10

Cabbage Palm *(Sabal palmetto)*
zones 7 to 10

Mahogany *(Swietenia mahagoni)*
zone 10

Red Mulberry *(Morus rubra)*
zones 5 to 10

Blolly *(Guapira discolor)* zone 10

Shortleaf Fig *(Ficus citrifolia)* zone 10

*Shrubs and Small Trees*

Myrsine *(Myrsine floridana)* zone 10

Lignum Vitae *(Guaiacum sanctum)*
zone 10

Satinleaf *(Chrysophyllum oliviforme)*
zone 10

Wild Coffee *(Psychotria nervosa)*
zones 9 to 10

Fire Bush *(Hamelia patens)*
zones 9 to 10

Florida Privet *(Forestiera segregata)*
zones 8 to 10

Sea Lavender *(Argusia gnaphalodes
[Mallotonia gnaphalodes])* zone 10

Inkberry *(Scaevola plumieri)*
zones 9 to 10

Pigeon Berry *(Bourreria succulenta)*
zone 10

Bay Cedar *(Suriana maritima)* zone 10

*Groundcovers and Vines*

Purple Muhly Grass *(Muhlenbergia capillaris)* zones 5 to 10

Beach Pea *(Canavalia rosea)*
zones 9 to 10

Sand Cordgrass *(Spartina bakeri)*
zones 8 to 10

Coontie *(Zamia pumila)* zones 9 to 10

Gopher Apple *(Licania michauxii)*
zones 8 to 10

Beach Sunflower *(Helianthus debilis)*
zones 8 to 10

Tickseed *(Coreopsis leavenworthii)*
zones 8 to 10

Milkweed *(Asclepias tuberosa)*
zones 5 to 10

SOUTH FLORIDA

Female cardinal on bittersweet

# The Prairies and Plains

## BY RICHARD THOM

*Amelanchier arborea*

**DOWNY SERVICEBERRY**

The fruits of this attractive tree are consumed by more than 30 species of birds. Plants can grow to 40' and spread about half their height, but are usually much smaller, sometimes forming a multi-stemmed shrub. Silver-gray bark is smooth to slightly furrowed. Foliage turns pale orange and yellow in fall.

**NATIVE HABITAT:** Woods, bluffs, and rocky glades.

**USDA HARDINESS ZONES:** 3 to 8.

**FLOWERS AND FRUIT:** Showy white flowers, produced in clusters near the branch tips, often develop before leaves. The sweet, rounded, purple fruits resemble blueberries. One of the earliest native trees to blossom in midwestern woodlands; fruits ripen by early summer and are quickly eaten by wildlife and people.

**HOW TO GROW:** Downy serviceberry grows well in shade to full sun, and in moist to dry, well-drained soils. Best growth is on deep, fertile soils with best flower and fruit production in full sun or light shade. A good specimen tree in the home landscape.

**BIRDS ATTRACTED:** Gray Catbird, chickadees, American Crow, orioles, American Robin, Brown Thrasher, thrushes, Tufted Titmouse, Northern Cardinal, Rose-breasted Grosbeak, Eastern Kingbird, Scarlet Tanager, Hairy Woodpecker, and Northern Flicker.

**ALTERNATIVES:** Saskatoon serviceberry *(Amelanchier alnifolia)* is native to the northern Great Plains, growing in moist to dry soils and often forming thickets. Wildlife values are similar to those of downy serviceberry. Zones 3 to 4.

*Buchloe dactyloides*

**BUFFALOGRASS**

This perennial, warm-season grass provides nest material, food in the form of seeds, and cover for many bird species. During the growing season, the grass is a soft, bluish green color, turning golden brown when dormant. Buffalograss grows to only 6" to 12" and spreads by above-ground runners to form a dense turf. Its short height lends it to areas where a "mowed" look is desirable.

**NATIVE HABITAT:** Prairies of the Great Plains.

**USDA HARDINESS ZONES:** 3 to 7

**FLOWERS AND FRUIT:** Yellowish green flowers form on spikelets above the grass leaves throughout the growing season. Seeds follow shortly after flow-

Buffalograss (*Buchloe dactyloides*) offers abundant seeds that birds eat.

ering. This warm-season grass is active when soil temperatures rise in late spring.

**HOW TO GROW:** Grow from seed in full sun on well-drained soils. Once established, buffalograss is drought-resistant and needs little or no watering. It is an excellent, low-maintenance groundcover.

**BIRDS ATTRACTED:** Buffalograss offers nest materials for birds with fine nest linings. Sparrows, finches, and other birds eat the seeds. The turf provides low cover for many species and habitat for insects and small mammals.

**ALTERNATIVES:** Sideoats gramma grass *(Bouteloua curtipendula)* is a bunch-forming prairie grass that can be grown in full sun to light shade on most soils. Can be planted with wildflowers in a native plant garden or as a specimen plant. It grows 12" to 24" high. Zones 3 to 8.

*Celtis occidentalis*
**HACKBERRY**
Hackberry is an excellent yard tree that provides late-season fruits for many birds as well as nesting sites and shelter. Small to large trees are fast-growing, with a spreading, rounded crown and straight trunk with gray bark.

PRAIRIES & PLAINS

Hackberry (*Celtis occidentalis*)

**BIRDS ATTRACTED:** Winter-persistent fruits provide late-season food for many birds, including Cedar Waxwing, Northern Mockingbird, Northern Cardinal, Yellow-bellied Sapsucker, thrushes, American Robin, sparrows, quail, and Wild Turkey. Hackberry also provides insects, nest sites, and shelter for many species.

**ALTERNATIVES:** Netted hackberry (*Celtis reticulata*) is a small tree that tolerates drier conditions; it is native to the southwestern plains. Sugarberry (*Celtis laevigata*), a medium-sized tree native to the southeast part of the region, grows in lowlands and tolerates clay soil.

Leaves turn bright yellow in fall.
**NATIVE HABITAT:** Adapted to a wide range of soils and moisture from flood plains to rocky hills. Native to most of the region.
**USDA HARDINESS ZONES:** 3 to 8
**FLOWERS AND FRUIT:** Small flowers bloom in spring on hanging stalks; fruits—rounded, fleshy, purple to orange—ripen in early fall and can persist on trees until well into winter.
**HOW TO GROW:** Plant in full sun or light shade in most soils, but grows best on deep, rich soils. Hackberry is drought-resistant, free of most pests and diseases, a good specimen tree, and also works well in windbreaks.

*Cornus drummondii*
**ROUGH-LEAVED DOGWOOD**
Many bird species are attracted to rough-leaved dogwood for its food, cover, and nest sites. This thicket-forming shrub or small, spreading tree grows to 20' and has a narrow, irregular crown.
**NATIVE HABITAT:** Roadsides, fencerows, rocky glades, woodland margins, and streamsides in all types of soil.
**USDA HARDINESS ZONES:** 4 to 8
**FLOWERS AND FRUIT:** Abundant small, yellowish flowers borne in clusters develop into white, berry-like fruit. Flowers are fragrant, but some people dislike their slightly fetid odor. Flowers

Rough-leaved dogwood

Flicker, thrushes, vireos, kingbirds, and Cedar Waxwing. Other birds forage for insects in its branches.

**ALTERNATIVES:** Gray dogwood *(Cornus racemosa)* is a thicket-forming shrub to 12', similar in wildlife value to rough-leaved dogwood; zones 3 to 7. Red-osier dogwood *(Cornus stolonifera)*, is native to the northern U.S. and Canada. Its branches turn a striking red in the fall and winter; zones 3 to 8. Silky dogwood *(Cornus amomum)* is a small, thicket-forming dogwood of streamsides, low woods, spring branches, and other moist areas. Branches turn reddish in winter, and the fruits are blue; zones 4 to 9.

appear in late spring; fruit matures in late summer to early fall and remains on branches until eaten by wildlife.

**HOW TO GROW:** This plant is cold- and drought-tolerant and grows well in sun or partial shade in all types of soil. Rough-leaved dogwood can spread by underground stems to form thickets. Plant as an informal hedge, as part of a windbreak, or in a back corner where there is room for it to spread and provide the most value to wildlife.

**BIRDS ATTRACTED:** More than 40 species of birds eat the fruit, including quail, Wild Turkey, Northern Cardinal, American Robin, Eastern Bluebird, Brown Thrasher, Gray Catbird, Northern

*Corylus americana*
**HAZELNUT**

Many species use this shrub for food, while others use it for cover and nest sites. Hazelnut is a somewhat coarse-looking, rapid-growing, multiple-stemmed shrub that forms dense clumps or thickets, rarely exceeding 10' in height. Its leaves turn golden and orange in fall.

**NATIVE HABITAT:** Open woods, woodland borders, fencerows, and roadsides over most of the region.

**USDA HARDINESS ZONES:** 3 to 8

**FLOWERS AND FRUIT:** Male flowers are catkins; female flowers are star-like tufts. Fruits are small, brown, edible

**PRAIRIES & PLAINS**

Hazelnut (*Corylus americana*)

nuts enclosed in ragged-edged husks. Plants flower from February to April; fruits form from July to September, persisting into winter if not eaten first.

**HOW TO GROW:** Grows in full sun to partial shade on dry to moist, well-drained soils. Best given enough space to form an informal hedge, screen, or thicket, or incorporate into a windbreak. Tolerates even poor, gravelly soils.

**BIRDS ATTRACTED:** Ruffed Grouse and Wild Turkey eat the buds, catkins, and fruit; Red-bellied and Hairy Woodpecker and Blue Jay relish the nuts; many species use the dense leaves and branches for cover and nest sites.

**ALTERNATIVES:** Beaked hazelnut *(Cory-lus cornuta)* is similar in growth habit and wildlife value but tolerates greater shade. Native to northern parts of the region; Zones 2 to 8.

*Echinacea pallida*
**PALE PURPLE CONEFLOWER**
Seed-eating species of birds are drawn to this member of the daisy family. It is an attractive, drought-resistant, long-lived perennial wildflower with stiff, erect stems to about 3' tall and spreads to form clumps.

**NATIVE HABITAT:** Prairies, glades, and open woodlands in the eastern part of the region.

**USDA HARDINESS ZONES:** 3 to 7

**FLOWERS AND FRUIT:** Each stem bears a large, showy, pink to pale purple blossom with drooping, petal-like ray flowers about 3" long. The fruits form in the central cone, like a small sunflower. Blooms from late spring to midsummer. Fruits mature in late summer and early fall, persisting on the stems into winter.

**HOW TO GROW:** Can be grown from seed or from nursery-raised, bare-root or container stock. Plant in mixtures with native prairie grasses or as accents or bedding plants. Grow in full sun or very light shade in any well-drained soil.

**BIRDS ATTRACTED:** The small seeds are relished by American Goldfinch, Pine Siskin, sparrows, and many other seed-eating species. Additionally, the flowers

PRAIRIES & PLAINS

Fritillary on *Echinacea pallida*

attract bees, butterflies, and other insects. Many species find refuge and cover in the stiff plants.

**ALTERNATIVES**: Narrow-leaved prairie coneflower *(Echinacea angustifolia)* is a look-alike relative native to the central and western Great Plains. It is extremely drought-tolerant once established; Zones 3 to 7. Purple coneflower *(Echinacea purpurea)* is deeper purple and wider-leaved. Several cultivars of this favorite garden wildflower are available. Although less drought-tolerant, purple coneflower is more tolerant of shady sites; Zones 3 to 7. Tall gayfeather or prairie blazing star *(Liatris pycnostachya)* and other *Liatris* species are also striking wildflowers in the daisy family. They have clusters of purple flowers on slender plants up to 5' tall. Wildlife values are similar to those of the coneflowers; Zones 3 to 8.

## *Juniperus virginiana*
### EASTERN RED CEDAR

Red cedar, the most widespread conifer of eastern North America, provides nest sites, fruit, associated insects, and winter cover to a variety of birds. Trees can live more than 300 years and grow to 60' tall, but are usually smaller with variable shape, from pyramidal to rounded to columnar. There is much regional variation and many selections and varieties are available.

**NATIVE HABITAT**: Fencerows, old fields, open woods, rocky glades, and cliffs in a wide range of soils.

**USDA HARDINESS ZONES**: 3 to 9

**FLOWERS AND FRUIT**: Male and female cones grow on separate trees. Berry-like fruits are at first whitish, then light green, and finally turn dark blue. Large seed crops occur every second or third year on any given female tree. Trees bloom March to May. Fruit matures from September to November and persists through the winter, unless eaten by wildlife.

**HOW TO GROW**: Easily transplanted, red cedar grows in full sun or light shade in most soils. Use red cedar in windbreaks on the north and west sides of your property, in hedges or informal screens, or as specimen trees.

**BIRDS ATTRACTED**: Red cedar provides excellent nesting habitat for many species, such as Brown Thrasher and Mourning Dove. The fruit is eaten by

PRAIRIES & PLAINS

over 30 species, including Eastern Blue-bird, Cedar Waxwing, American Robin, Yellow-rumped Warbler, Purple and House Finch, and sparrows. Warblers and kinglets glean insects from the evergreen foliage, which also provides winter cover.

ALTERNATIVES: Nurseries may have local or specially adapted stock. The female cultivar 'Canaertii' has deep-green needles and bluish fruit. Ashe juniper *(Juniperus ashei)*, a small tree native to the southern part of the region, grows best on soils underlain by limestone. It has a short trunk and rounded crown and often branches close to the ground; Zones 6 to 8. Com-mon juniper *(Juniperus communis)* is a medium to large evergreen shrub avail-able in many varieties and cultivars; useful as a groundcover, hedge, or specimen. Bluish, waxy fruits are val-ued by the same species as those that feed on the fruits of red cedar; Zones 3 to 8.

*Parthenocissus quinquefolia*
**VIRGINIA CREEPER**
Many birds take refuge in the cover of this dense, woody, climbing vine while others eat the fruit. Also grows as a groundcover, sometimes forming dense masses. Virginia creeper climbs tall trees and walls, as high as its support allows, and is especially attractive in fall

when its leaves turn deep scarlet.
NATIVE HABITAT: Woods, thickets, fencerows, streamsides, and bluffs of the eastern plains.
USDA HARDINESS ZONES: 3 to 9
FLOWERS AND FRUIT: Inconspicuous greenish flowers form in clusters that develop into small, dark-purple, berry-like fruits. Flowers appear from late spring through summer; fruit from Sep-tember to October.
HOW TO GROW: Adapted to sun or shade and most soil and moisture con-ditions. Grows best in moist, rich soil and full sun. Plant where it can climb a fence, tree, or wall; or as a groundcover

Virginia creeper

The wild plum is a showy backyard shrub where birds can find insects to eat.

in full sun or light shade.

**BIRDS ATTRACTED:** Many birds benefit from this vine's cover; others like to eat the fruit, including Eastern Bluebird, Gray Catbird, chickadees, American Crow, Northern Flicker, Great-crested Flycatcher, Northern Mockingbird, White-breasted Nuthatch, thrushes, Tufted Titmouse, woodpeckers, Wild Turkey, and Bobwhite.

**ALTERNATIVES:** Woodbine *(Parthenocissus vitacea)* is a very similar species; its natural range extends farther north and west than that of Virginia creeper, through most of the Great Plains. Woodbine is less of a climber and more of a sprawler and groundcover.

*Prunus americana*
**WILD PLUM**

Many bird species are drawn to the wild plum for cover, nest, and insect-foraging sites. There are many selections of this species, which ranges in habit from small tree with spreading crown to thicket-forming shrub with multiple stems; it is rarely taller than 25'.

**NATIVE HABITAT:** Woods, pastures, fencerows, roadsides, and old fields throughout the Northern Plains.

**USDA HARDINESS ZONES:** 3 to 9

**FLOWERS AND FRUIT:** White, fragrant, showy flowers often appear before leaves are fully developed. Globe-

PRAIRIES & PLAINS

shaped, yellow-orange or reddish fruit is up to 1" long. Leaves turn yellow, orange, and red in fall. One of the first woody plants to bloom in the spring. Fruit matures from July to September.

**HOW TO GROW:** This fast-growing, drought-resistant species grows in full sun or light shade in well-drained, moist to dry soils. Plant as an individual tree or closely space several plants to form a plum thicket.

**BIRDS ATTRACTED:** Among the species that use the wild plum for cover and nest and insect-foraging sites are Brown Thrasher, Northern Mockingbird, and Rufous-sided Towhee. The large fruits are used more by mammals than birds, but birds are attracted to the insects that use this plant.

**ALTERNATIVES:** Because of its attractiveness as a yard plant, many selections of wild plum have been propagat-

Acorn of bur oak

ed; look for locally adapted cultivars. Big tree plum *(Prunus mexicana)* is similar to American wild plum but with a more southern distribution. This drought-resistant plum has edible fruit and grows as an individual tree rather than forming thickets; Zones 7 to 9. Chickasaw plum *(Prunus angustifolia)* is widely distributed in the southern half of the region, often forming thickets. Bears red to yellow fruit up to ½" long; Zones 6 to 9.

---

*Quercus macrocarpa*
**BUR OAK**
This long-lived tree—200 to 300 years—feeds and houses many animals; birds use it for cover, cavities, nest sites, acorns, and insects. Bur oak, an attractive street and yard tree, is medium to large with a broad, rounded crown and tall, straight trunk.

**NATIVE HABITAT:** Moist bottomland forests to dry uplands and prairie groves, from the Great Plains east through the central and north central U.S.

**USDA HARDINESS ZONES:** 3 to 8

**FLOWERS AND FRUIT:** Inconspicuous flowers are produced in spring on reddish and yellow-green catkins. The fruit, a large acorn with an unusual, fringed cup, matures by the end of the growing season.

**HOW TO GROW:** Grows well in full sun

to light shade. Tolerates a wide range of soil and moisture conditions. Prefers deep, moist, well-drained soil, but tolerates much drier soil. Bur oak makes an excellent yard, street, or specimen tree.

**BIRDS ATTRACTED:** Nearly 100 wildlife species have been documented to use this tree. Warblers and other spring and fall migrants collect insects from its leaves and branches and use it for cover, cavities, and nest sites. Blue Jay, Red-headed Woodpecker, Wood Duck, grouse, and Wild Turkey eat the acorns.

**ALTERNATIVES:** Chinkapin oak *(Quercus muehlenbergii),* native to central and southern parts of the plains, is a medium-sized tree that tolerates dry conditions. Post oak *(Quercus stellata),* native to the southern part of the region, is a small to medium tree that tolerates a wide range of soil conditions; shiny, leathery leaves turn red in fall. There are many other native oak species with a wide range of growth characteristics. All produce acorns, which would attract the species that eat this type of fruit, and all provide some degree of cover, as well as nesting and insect-foraging opportunities.

---

*Rhus glabra*
## SMOOTH SUMAC
Many birds seek out sumac thickets for nest sites, cover, and insects; some birds consume the fruits in winter,

Brown Thrasher on smooth sumac

when other food sources are depleted. This fast-growing shrub has foliage that turns vivid scarlet in fall. It often forms wide clumps or thickets.

**NATIVE HABITAT:** Clearings, abandoned fields, prairies, pastures, woodland edges, fencerows, and roadsides throughout the Plains.

**USDA HARDINESS ZONES:** 3 to 9

**FLOWERS AND FRUIT:** Male and female flowers are on different plants; flowers of both sexes are inconspicuous, although they attract many insects; only female plants produce the dense, showy clusters of bright red fruit. Flowers appear in the spring; fruits form in late summer and fall and persist on the plant into winter.

PRAIRIES & PLAINS

PRAIRIES & PLAINS

**HOW TO GROW**: Smooth sumac does best in full sun and with enough space to form a dense grouping. Plant as part of a windbreak, informal screen, or clump. Sumac tolerates a wide range of soil conditions, wind, and drought.

**BIRDS ATTRACTED**: Sumac fruit is not preferred by most species, but is available as winter survival fare. Birds that eat sumac fruit include Prairie Chicken, Ring-necked Pheasant, Bobwhite Quail, Wild Turkey, Eastern Bluebird, Northern Cardinal, Brown Thrasher, American Robin, Yellow-rumped Warbler, Purple Finch, and Red-headed Woodpecker. Sumac thickets also provide nest sites, cover, and insect-foraging areas for many species.

**ALTERNATIVES**: Shining sumac *(Rhus copallina)*, a native of the Southern Plains, is similar to smooth sumac. Its leaves turn brilliant red to red-orange in fall; Zones 4 to 9.

---

*Viburnum rufidulum*
**RUSTY HAW**

Many birds eat the fruits of this shrub or small tree. Its attractive, shiny leaves have a "lacquered" look, and turn purple to red in fall. It is seldom taller than 20', and has an open, irregular crown.

**NATIVE HABITAT**: Woods, prairie edges, streamsides, glades, and thickets of the southern Plains.

**USDA HARDINESS ZONES**: 5 to 9

Rusty haw (*Viburnum rufidulum*)

**HOW TO GROW**: Grows well in full sun or partial shade and dry to moist, well-drained soils. Plant as a single specimen tree, as part of a group, or along an edge.

**FLOWERS AND FRUIT**: Numerous small, white flowers form showy, flat clusters up to 6" across. Flowers develop into fleshy, dark purple fruits. Rusty haw blooms in late spring and fruits mature in September and October.

**BIRDS ATTRACTED**: Many birds eat the fruit, including Wild Turkey, Ruffed Grouse, Eastern Bluebird, Cedar Waxwing, Northern Flicker, Pileated Woodpecker, Northern Mockingbird, Gray Catbird, American Robin, Brown Thrasher, and Purple Finch.

**ALTERNATIVES**: Nannyberry *(Viburnum*

lentago) is a large viburnum, occasionally growing to 20-plus feet. Similar to rusty haw in landscape use and birds attracted. Adapted to the Northern Plains, Zones 2 to 7.

## MORE GREAT BIRD PLANTS FOR THE PRAIRIES AND PLAINS

### Trees

Green Ash *(Fraxinus pennsylvanica)* zones 2 to 9

Pecan *(Carya illinoensis)* zones 6 to 9

Persimmon *(Diospyros virginiana)* zones 5 to 9

Red Mulberry *(Morus rubra)* zones 4 to 9

River Birch *(Betula nigra)* zones 4 to 9

### Shrubs and Small Trees

Common Chokecherry *(Prunus virginiana)* zones 3 to 5

Buffalo Berry *(Shepherdia argentea)* zones 2 to 6

Deciduous Holly *(Ilex decidua)* zones 5 to 9

Elderberry *(Sambucus canadensis)* zones 3 to 7

Flowering Crabs (*Malus* species) Note: Select locally adapted cultivars with small, winter-persistent fruits and resistance to fire blight and cedar-apple rust diseases; zones 3 to 9

Fragant Sumac *(Rhus aromatica)* zones 3 to 9

Fringe Tree *(Chionanthus virginicus)* zones 5 to 9

Hawthorns *(Crateagus* species) see Flowering Crabs; zones 3 to 9

Missouri Gooseberry *(Ribes missouriense)* zones 3 to 6

Native Blackberries and Raspberries (*Rubus* species) zones 4 to 7

Prairie Rose *(Rosa arkansana)* zones 3 to 7

Texas Madrone *(Arbutus texana)* zones 7 to 8

Western Snowberry *(Symphoricarpos occidentalis)* zones 3 to 6

Western Soapberry *(Sapindus drumondii)* zones 5 to 7

Woolly Buckthorn, Chittim Wood *(Bumelia lanuginosa)* zones 6 to 9

### Groundcovers and Vines

Trumpet Creeper *(Campsis radicans)* zones 4 to 9

Wild Grapes *(Vitus* species) zones 3 to 7

Creeping Juniper *(Juniperus horizontalis)* zones 2 to 9

### Grasses and Wildflowers

Butterfly Weed *(Asclepias tuberosa)* zones 3 to 7

Little Bluestem Grass *(Schizachyrium scoparium)* zones 5 to 8

Native Asters (*Aster* species) zones 3 to 7

Native Sunflowers (*Helianthus* species) zones 3 to 7

Narrow-leaved Prairie Coneflower *(Echinacea angustifolia)* zones 3 to 7

# The Western Mountains and Deserts

## BY BETH HUNING

*Alnus rhombifolia*
**WHITE ALDER**

White alder provides food for mountain and migrating birds, as well as cover, nesting, and roosting habitat. Trees can grow from 30' to 115' tall and thrive in coastal areas.

**NATIVE HABITAT:** Swampy ground, stream courses, and river banks, often at water's edge, sometimes in densely forested areas.

**USDA HARDINESS ZONES:** 7 to 9

**FLOWERS AND FRUIT:** Trees produce both male and female flowers; the female flowers develop into cone-like catkins that dangle from the tree year-round. Tiny seeds are abundant on these catkins during winter and spring and are an important food source for mountain and migrating birds.

**HOW TO GROW:** Plant in moist areas. White alder does well in sun but tolerates shade quite well. White alder and its close relative red alder *(Alnus rubra)* occupy similar habitats in the wild; they can be used interchangeably. Although they naturally grow along stream courses, they are easily cultivated and fast-growing in garden settings, and will rapidly grow into shade trees if water is available and the growing sea-son is relatively long.

**BIRDS ATTRACTED:** Pine Siskin, grosbeaks, and Purple Finch eat the seeds and fruit. The tree also provides cover, and nesting and roosting habitat for warblers.

**ALTERNATIVES:** Arizona alder *(Alnus oblongifolia)* and mountain alder *(Alnus incana* subsp. *tenuifolia)* are very closely related to white and red alders and have comparable wildlife values, as do any number of native trees in the birch family (Betulaceae).

*Arctostaphylos pungens*
**MANZANITA**

There are about 50 species of manzanita, a common western shrub, many of them attractive ornamentals that also provide shelter and food for wildlife. *Arctostaphylos pungens* is a dense, woody shrub with smooth, deep-red bark and thick, waxy, oval leaves. It generally grows 3' or more in height, although related species can be more prostrate in habit.

**NATIVE HABITAT:** Open hillsides and yellow pine forests up to about 6,000'.

**USDA HARDINESS ZONES:** 8 to 9

**FLOWERS AND FRUIT:** Small clusters of white or pink bell-shaped flowers bloom in spring and early summer, developing into small red berries in summer and early fall.

HOW TO GROW: An attractive, drought-tolerant shrub, manzanita thrives in dry, well-drained soil in open sun, but can do well in a variety of soils; prefers sun to partial shade. When planted from nursery stock, manzanita quickly develops into a shrub or groundcover.

BIRDS ATTRACTED: Provides cover and food for grouse, quail, and other low-nesting and ground-feeding birds, including towhees.

ALTERNATIVES: Greenleaf manzanita *(Arctostaphylos patula)*, common manzanita *(Arctostaphylos manzanita)*, and pinemat manzanita *(Arctostaphylos nevadensis*, a prostrate species and good groundcover) can be used interchangeably with *Arctostaphylos pungens*, as they have similar wildlife values.

---

*Atriplex lentiformis*
## QUAILBUSH
One of several species known as saltbush, this shrub can be pruned to form a hedge 6' to 10' tall.

NATIVE HABITAT: Desert Southwest and California, growing in dense patches in saline areas.

USDA HARDINESS ZONES: 6 to 9

FLOWERS AND FRUIT: Dry, hard, one-seeded fruits develop from small, nondescript flowers. Fruits develop in the fall and throughout the winter.

HOW TO GROW: Prefers dry conditions, well-drained soils, and full sun, making this an excellent drought-tolerant shrub for arid climates. Deciduous in dry areas. When several plants are clustered and pruned to prevent the plants from becoming too woody, quailbush will develop into an excellent hedge.

BIRDS ATTRACTED: Quail and other ground-dwelling species, such as

Quailbush *(Atriplex lentiformis)*

towhees, find cover and nest among the branches. Twenty-nine species of birds, including doves, phoebes, and gnatcatchers, are known to feed on the fruit of this and related saltbush species.

ALTERNATIVES: Desert saltbush *(Atriplex polycarpa)*; desert holly *(A. hymenelytra)* are related species of saltbush that provide comparable food and habitat values.

MOUNTAINS & DESERTS

MOUNTAINS &
DESERTS

Desert willow (*Chilopsis linearis*) attracts many species of hummingbirds.

*Chilopsis linearis*
**DESERT WILLOW**

This plant's common name derives from its elliptical leaves, which resemble those of true willows *(Salix* species), but desert willow does not produce the same type of flower. Hummingbirds are drawn to the blossoms of this quick-growing plant, which often develops a full, spreading, shrub-like form, as broad as it is high.

**NATIVE HABITAT:** Open areas and stream courses of deserts, and the basin and ranges of the southwestern U.S.

**USDA HARDINESS ZONES:** 7 to 9

**FLOWERS AND FRUIT:** Trumpet-shaped flowers, generally purplish to pink, appear in late spring through late summer, depending upon elevation and exposure to sun. Desert willow fruit is a pod-like capsule.

**HOW TO GROW:** Sometimes used in garden settings as a spreading tree; thrives in direct sun in dry, open areas. Is drought-tolerant and hence deciduous from late summer through mid-winter.

**BIRDS ATTRACTED:** Nectar in trumpet-shaped flowers attracts a variety of Southwestern hummingbirds, including Black-chinned, Costa's, and Broad-tailed.

**ALTERNATIVES:** Although not related, flowering currant *(Ribes sanguineum)* and other shrub-like *Ribes* species also attract hummingbirds to the flowers and other birds to the fruit.

*Fragaria vesca* subsp. *californica*
**WILD STRAWBERRY**

This hardy, perennial herbaceous groundcover produces fruits that birds and people enjoy. It is a tightly growing groundcover with stems 4" to 5" long that often act as runners, producing new plantlets.

**NATIVE HABITAT:** Shaded, damp places on forest floors in foothills, and yellow pine belts of the western mountains, below 7,000'.

**USDA HARDINESS ZONES:** 7 to 9

**FLOWERS AND FRUIT:** Wild strawberry is a member of the rose family; its white flowers grow in clusters, each flower with 5 small petals, giving it the appearance of a tiny rose. In late spring and early summer, flowers develop into tiny red strawberries that are consumed by numerous species of birds and other wildlife.

**HOW TO GROW:** Plant this hardy groundcover in sunny or shaded areas. Although it thrives with a regular source of moisture, especially during the blooming and fruiting periods, it will tolerate intermittent dryness and rebound successfully.

**BIRDS ATTRACTED:** Many species of birds are attracted to the delicious fruit. These include California and Mountain Quail, waxwings, grouse, Northern Mockingbird, California and Spotted Towhee, American Robin, Pine and

**MOUNTAINS & DESERTS**

Black-headed Grosbeak, Scrub Jay, Song Sparrow, and other sparrows.
**ALTERNATIVES:** Although not all are native to the West, several other wild strawberries *(Fragaria* species) can be found in nurseries. These include wood strawberry *(Fragaria vesca* subsp. *bracteata),* Virginia strawberry *(Fragaria virginiana),* and beach strawberry *(Fragaria chiloensis).*

Colorado blue spruce *(Picea pungens)*

## *Picea pungens*
### COLORADO BLUE SPRUCE

This stately tree provides seeds, harbors grubs and insects under its bark, and serves as a roosting and nesting site for a wide variety of western birds. It is a slow-growing coniferous tree that can reach 150'.

**NATIVE HABITAT:** Rocky Mountains.

**USDA HARDINESS ZONES:** 3 to 5

**FLOWERS AND FRUIT:** Seeds are produced at the base of the papery scales of cones.

**HOW TO GROW:** This slow-growing coniferous tree is good for borders, edges of gardens, or wherever shade is desired. Plant in well-drained soil; blue spruce prefers full sun but will tolerate light shade.

**BIRDS ATTRACTED:** Seeds provide food for a variety of mountain birds, including Scrub and Steller's Jay, chickadees, grosbeaks, finches, Pine Siskin, and sparrows. Insects in the bark attract nuthatches, Brown Creeper, Nashville Warbler, and other warblers. The tree also offers perching habitat for Olive-sided Flycatcher and other flycatchers.

**ALTERNATIVES:** Although not directly related, western hemlock *(Tsuga heterophylla),* Engelmann spruce *(Picea engelmannii),* red fir *(Abies magnifica),* and white fir *(Abies concolor)* can also provide seed for the mountain and migratory birds listed above.

MOUNTAINS & DESERTS

*Pinus ponderosa*
## PONDEROSA PINE
*Pinus jeffreyi*
## JEFFREY PINE

Both pines provide seeds, harbor grubs and insects under their bark, and serve as roosting and nesting sites for many western birds. When mature, these trees range from 60' to 200' high, and up to 7' in trunk diameter.

**NATIVE HABITAT:** Both trees are native to sunny sides of western mountains and occupy dry, sandy soils. Ponderosa pines tend to colonize the edges of forests at mid-elevations, while Jeffrey pines are most common between 6,000' and 9,000', often occupying rock slopes and eastern escarpments of western mountain ranges.

**USDA HARDINESS ZONES:** 5 to 7

**FLOWERS AND FRUIT:** When they are about 20 years old, trees will produce seeds in cones. The cones mature in two years, shedding seeds in the summer and fall of the second year. Jeffrey pine cones and seeds are both larger than those of the ponderosa pine.

**HOW TO GROW:** Both pines will grow most successfully when planted in full sun. Both also prefer well-drained soil and dry conditions. Because, like many cold-climate pines, they are slow-growing, consider purchasing larger tree

MOUNTAINS & DESERTS

Lodgepole pine provides seeds for birds to eat and roosting places.

forms. When mature, these trees will provide good shade.

BIRDS ATTRACTED: The seeds of these pines are an important food source for Steller's Jay, tanagers, grosbeaks, Purple, Cassin's, and House Finch, Pine Siskin, and sparrows. Bark harbors grubs and insects that provide food for Common Flicker, Lewis's, Nuttall's, and White-headed Woodpecker, White and Red-breasted Nuthatch, and Brown Creeper. Provides roosting and nesting sites for raptors, especially Great Horned, Screech, and Pygmy Owl.

ALTERNATIVES: Sugar pine *(Pinus lambertiana)*, lodgepole pine *(P. murrayana)*, digger pine *(P. sabiniana)*, and pinon pine *(P. monophylla)* all produce seeds that the birds listed above will eat; these birds will also use these trees for roosting. Sugar pines are taller than lodgepole and digger pines and have longer branches.

*Prosopis velutina*
### MESQUITE

Mesquite, a bushy, thorny-branched shrub, provides nutritious seeds for birds and other wildlife, as well as cover and nest sites in its low-growing branches.

NATIVE HABITAT: California deserts below 5,000', wherever groundwater can be

MOUNTAINS & DESERTS

Mesquite (*Prosopis velutina*) offers birds seeds, cover, and nesting sites.

tapped by this plant's extensive root system.

**USDA HARDINESS ZONES:** 8 to 10

**FLOWERS AND FRUIT:** Produces small yellow blossoms in the spring that, in late spring and summer, mature into bean pods containing nutritious seeds for birds and other wildlife.

**HOW TO GROW:** Prefers dry, sunny locations with well-drained soil; water intermittently if moisture is not available from a source of groundwater. Provides good cover and border habitat.

**BIRDS ATTRACTED:** Gambel's Quail; Mourning, White-winged, Common Ground, and Inca Dove; Ladder-backed Woodpecker; Black-chinned, Broad-tailed, and Costa's Hummingbird; Ash-throated Flycatcher; Say's and Black Phoebe; Scrub Jay; Verdin; Bushtit; Blue-gray and Black-tailed Gnatcatcher; Loggerhead Shrike; Curved-bill Thrasher; Phainopepla; Lucy's Warbler; Pyrrhuloxia; Green-tailed Towhee; Song, Black-throated, and Cassin's Finch; Sage Sparrow and other sparrow species; and Western Meadowlark.

**ALTERNATIVES:** Screwbean mesquite *(Prosopis pubescens)* and catclaw *(Acacia greggii)* are related species that produce seeds similar to those of mesquite.

---

*Ribes sanguineum*
## FLOWERING CURRANT
Hummingbirds are attracted to the blossoms of this shrub, while many

Flowering currant (*Ribes sanguineum*)

other birds consume the fruits. Bushes can grow to about 6' and can be pruned into a dense hedge.

**NATIVE HABITAT:** Foothill and forested mountain slopes to about 6,000', generally in moist or damp areas, or hillsides along creeks.

**USDA HARDINESS ZONES:** 6 to 8

**FLOWERS AND FRUIT:** Attractive red tubular flowers develop into clusters of spherical black fruits containing small seeds. Blooms in the spring, developing fruits in summer. Both seeds and fruits are an attractive food source for birds.

**HOW TO GROW:** Easily grown in a backyard, this attractive, hardy shrub is readily adaptable to a variety of settings. It is often used ornamentally in formal gardens. Prefers well-drained

MOUNTAINS & DESERTS

Coyote willow provides refuge and food for birds along streams and rivers.

soil and full sun but will grow in semi-shade for part of the day.

**BIRDS ATTRACTED:** Small clusters of pink or reddish flowers attract a variety of hummingbirds. Fruits of this and other wild currant species provide a source of food for mountain and desert birds, such as Northern Flicker, Hermit and Swainson's Thrush, Townsend's Solitaire, Western and Mountain Bluebird, and quail.

**ALTERNATIVES:** Wax currant *(Ribes cereum)*, buffalo currant *(R. odoratum)*, and golden currant *(R. aureum)* are other species of wild currants with similar fruits and food values.

*Salix exigua*
## COYOTE WILLOW

The dense cover provided by the coyote willow and other *Salix* species in natural habitats provides refuge and a source of insects for a large number of bird species in arid regions, particularly migratory birds. This tree-like shrub will grow to 15' in height.

**NATIVE HABITAT:** Along rivers and stream courses of the desert Southwest, creating densely forested river banks.

**USDA HARDINESS ZONES:** 8 to 9

**FLOWERS AND FRUIT:** Flowers grow in erect catkins, often called "pussy willows." Catkins bloom in spring before new leaves are produced; male and female flowers occur on different plants. Female catkin matures into capsules with tiny individual seeds, a source of food for birds. New trees can sprout from roots, stumps, or cuttings.

**HOW TO GROW:** Plant in moist, well-drained areas as border and cover in clumps or thickets. Does not tolerate deep shade. Like many willows, can be grown from cuttings.

**BIRDS ATTRACTED:** Yellow-bellied Sapsucker, Downy and Nuttall's Woodpecker, hummingbirds, Western and Cassin's Kingbird, Ash-throated Flycatcher, Bewick's Wren, warblers, orioles, blackbirds, White-crowned and Lincoln's Sparrow, goldfinches, and Cassin's Finch.

**ALTERNATIVES:** Other dense-growing willow species such as arroyo willow *(Salix lasiolepis)*, scouler or mountain willow *(S. scouleriana)*, pacific willow *(S. lucida* subsp. *lasiandra)*, or Lemmon willow *(S. lemmoni)*.

*Sambucus caerulea*
**BLUE ELDERBERRY**
The berries of this hardy deciduous shrub are eaten by a number of bird species. Plants are often tree-like, to 30', with long, brown branches and oblong leaves 1" to 6" long.

**NATIVE HABITAT:** From low elevations to the yellow pine belt in mountainous regions, most commonly on stream slopes.

**USDA HARDINESS ZONES:** 6 to 9

**FLOWERS AND FRUIT:** Clusters of small, cream-colored flowers develop into bunches of small juicy berries (¼") at tips of branches. Blooms in mid- to late spring with berries developing from late summer into fall.

**HOW TO GROW:** Plant this hardy, adaptable shrub in a sunny area, in fertile, moist soil.

**BIRDS ATTRACTED:** Berries are eaten by a variety of birds, including Mountain and California Quail, several species of woodpeckers, Western Kingbird, Black Phoebe, American Robin, Band-tailed Pigeon, and Black-headed Grosbeak.

**ALTERNATIVES:** The closely related American elderberry *(Sambucus canadensis)* is similar in appearance and grows in similar conditions, producing clusters of berries that are a food source for the species listed above.

Blue elderberry (*Sambucus caerulea*)

## *Vitis arizonica*
### CANYON GRAPE

This climbing vine—which uses other plants such as cottonwoods and willows as support and to gain access to direct sunlight—provides fruits for many birds. Stems will grow from 5' to 50', growing on other plants or on support structures.

**NATIVE HABITAT:** Canyons and water courses of the desert Southwest.

**USDA HARDINESS ZONES:** 7 to 9

**FLOWERS AND FRUIT:** Small branched clusters of fragrant green flowers ripen into clusters of grapes. Plants bloom in late spring and early summer, and grapes develop in mid-summer.

**HOW TO GROW:** Plant in sunny areas with well-drained soil. Provide a structure upon which the vine can climb, which it does quite rapidly. Canyon grape does well along walls, as a backdrop, or as a shade source for other plants.

**BIRDS ATTRACTED:** Many bird species feed on the fruits. Commonly attracted birds include several species of quail, Scrub Jay, Wrentit, Western Bluebird, Northern Mockingbird, and Cedar Waxwing.

**ALTERNATIVES:** California grape *(Vitis californica)* is a similar, closely related climbing vine occupying similar zones, and produces fruit that will attract any of the species listed above.

## MORE GREAT BIRD PLANTS FOR THE WESTERN MOUNTAINS AND DESERTS

*Trees*

Arizona Ash *(Fraxinus velutina)* zones 8 to 9

Cottonwood *(Populus fremontii)* zones 8 to 9

Horsebean Palo Verde *(Parkinsonia aculeata)* zones 8 to 10

Little Leaf Palo Verde *(Cercidium microphyllum)* zones 8 to 10

Pacific Dogwood *(Cornus nuttallii)* zones 8 to 9

Pinyon Pine *(Pinus monophylla)* zones 6 to 8

Rocky Mountain Juniper *(Juniperus scopulorum)* zones 5 to 7

Western Juniper *(Juniperus occidentalis)* zones 5 to 7

White Fir *(Abies concolor)* zones 7 to 8

*Shrubs*

Bitter Cherry *(Prunus emarginata)* zones 7 to 9

Brittlebush *(Encelia farinosa)* zones 8 to 10

Chokecherry *(Prunus virginiana)* zones 5 to 8

Creosote Bush *(Larrea tridentata)* zones 8 to 10

Oregon Grape *(Mahonia nervosa)* zones 8 to 9

Rocky Mountain Raspberry *(Rubus deliciosus)* zones 5 to 7

MOUNTAINS & DESERTS

Steller's Jay and other birds need dense shrubs for cover.

Serviceberry *(Amelanchier utahensis)*
    zones 5 to 8
Snowberry *(Symphoricarpos albus)*
    zones 4 to 7
Whitebark Raspberry *(Rubus
    leucodermis)* zones 5 to 7

*Groundcovers*
Beardtongues *(Penstemon* species,
    including *P. utahensis, P. eatonii,*
    and *P. barbatus)* zones 5 to 9
Cardinal Flower *(Lobelia cardinalis)*
    zones 7 to 9
Columbine *(Aquilegia pubescens)*
    zones 4 to 9
Common Sunflower *(Helianthus*

*annuus)* zones 5 to 9
Western Blueberry *(Vaccinium
    occidentale)* zones 4 to 8
Wild Buckwheats *(Eriogonum* species,
    including *E. ovalifolium, E. nudum*
    var. *nundum, E. compositum, E.
    parishii, E. saxatile)* zones 6 to 10

*Cacti*
Ocotillo *(Fouquieria splendens)*
    zones 9 to 10
Prickly Pear Cacti *(Opuntia* species,
    including *O. basilaris* [beavertail],
    *O. phaeacantha, O. chlorotica*
    [pancake pear], and *O. erinacea*
    [grizzly bear]) zones 9 to 10

MOUNTAINS & DESERTS

# The Pacific Coast

BY JESSE GRANTHAM

Desert honeysuckle, or flameflower

## *Anisacanthus thurberi*
### DESERT HONEYSUCKLE, FLAME-FLOWER

The blooms of this stiff-twigged, upright plant are favored by all western hummingbirds; plants will grow from 2' to 6'.

**NATIVE HABITAT:** Dry areas in Arizona, New Mexico, Texas, and northern Mexico.

**USDA HARDINESS ZONES:** 8 to 10

**FLOWERS AND FRUIT:** The 1½"-long, yellow-orange, tubular flowers are borne on spikes at the ends of branches. Some varieties have red flowers.

**HOW TO GROW:** Usually found in 1-gallon containers, most often in native plant nurseries. Does well in many soil types, from rich loam, to clay, to limestone. A drought-tolerant plant.

**BIRDS ATTRACTED:** A favorite of all western hummingbirds.

**ALTERNATIVES:** Several other *Anisacanthus* species native to the Southwest— *A. quadrifidus, A. linearis,* and *A. puberulus*—are worth trying in West Coast gardens.

## *Arbutus menziesii*
### PACIFIC MADRONE

The madrone is an important fall and early winter food source for many western birds. The main horticultural features of this fine tree are its beautiful, rusty-brown, smooth, and shiny bark and 3" to 5" green leaves, reminiscent of magnolia or bay laurel.

**NATIVE HABITAT:** Coastal ranges of the West, on open slopes to dark moist canyons, in rich, well-drained soils.

**USDA HARDINESS ZONE:** 9

**FLOWERS AND FRUIT:** Flowers are bell-shaped, pale pink to white, in clusters at the ends of the branches. In late October and November, the round, red to orange fruits are stunning and a favorite of birds.

**HOW TO GROW:** Pacific madrone grows broad and spreading in the open, and tall and slender in groves. It can be a large shrub to a rather large tree, ranging from 15' to over 80'. Madrone is very sensitive to root disturbance, so the novice gardener should proceed with caution—but the tree is well worth the effort when you succeed. Look for container plants that have well-developed root systems, so the soil won't fall away from the roots when transplanting. Madrones require rich, well-drained soils, with infrequent but thorough, deep watering during the summer months if planted in the spring. Fall-planted specimens require less water.

**BIRDS ATTRACTED:** Long-time residents of the habitat of madrone remember it as a favorite food source for Band-tailed

Pacific madrone (*Arbutus menziesii*)

Pigeon, whose numbers have declined. Other species that favor its fruit include Wild Turkey, California and Mountain Quail, most woodpeckers, American Robin, thrushes, and Purple, House, and Cassin's Finch. The finches pick at the fruits, as they are too large for them to ingest whole.

**ALTERNATIVES:** No similar alternatives.

## *Cornus nuttallii*
### MOUNTAIN DOGWOOD

The fruits of dogwoods ripen just as many birds are migrating in the fall, so these are an important food source. This dogwood grows straight and tall—up to 40 feet in open areas, while in dense shade it will become gracefully twisted and angular. It has a generally open habit with well-spaced, horizontal, slightly curving branches.

**NATIVE HABITAT:** Dense, moist woodlands on east- or north-facing slopes at higher elevations, in the foothills of the Coast Ranges, and mountains of the Pacific Northwest and northern California.

**USDA HARDINESS ZONES:** 8 to 9

**FLOWERS AND FRUIT:** A beautiful, graceful native of the West, this dogwood produces striking white bracts on bare branches before the leaves emerge; these bracts gleam in woodlands while other plants are putting forth fresh new foliage. Fruits are red and borne in clus-

PACIFIC COAST

ters in late September and October.

**HOW TO GROW:** You will have to search the native plant nurseries to find good specimens of this plant, but it will be worth the effort. Look for plants in deep tubes or 5-gallon containers, as trees grow better if their root systems are disturbed as little as possible. Plant in deep, rich soil, preferably in shady, open woodlands. Needs occasional watering in summer at lower elevations, even after established. A 5- to 10-gallon bucket with a small hole poked in the bottom, filled with water, and placed adjacent to the trunk will provide slow, deep watering in the absence of an irrigation system.

**BIRDS ATTRACTED:** Foragers include Band-tailed Pigeon, Wild Turkey, California and Mountain Quail, all the common western woodpeckers, American Robin, thrushes, vireos, tanagers, Black-headed Grosbeak, and all the finches except goldfinches and Pine Siskin.

**ALTERNATIVES:** Red-twig dogwood *(Cornus stolonifera)* is an important plant for migrant birds in the fall, from thrushes and vireos to grosbeaks and tanagers. Any fruits remaining after fall will be consumed by wintering woodpeckers, Hermit Thrush, and sparrows. Trees produce small, showy white flowers in spring and pale blue fruits in fall; they need moisture and grow best in full sun to light shade.

Mountain dogwood *(Cornus nuttallii)*

*Heteromeles arbutifolia*
## TOYON, CALIFORNIA HOLLY

Like the fruits of the hollies of the eastern U.S., toyon fruits ripen in late winter, just when food resources for many birds are dwindling. This medium to large shrub is evergreen, with an average height of 5' to 10', but in ideal situations it can reach 25'.

**NATIVE HABITAT:** Edges of oak woodlands, mixed pine-oak woodlands, and foothill chaparral of the Sierra Nevada and Coast Range mountains of California.

**USDA HARDINESS ZONES:** 8 to 10

**HOW TO GROW:** This is one of the more useful, but sometimes difficult, natives to transplant. It does not like to have its roots disturbed, and small plants are susceptible to root fungus and mildew. From containers, it is most successful if transplanted from a 5-gallon or larger pot, once it has a well-developed root system. Plant in deep, rich soil for best success and water infrequently but deeply the first summer.

**FLOWERS AND FRUIT:** Toyon flowers are white and in flat-topped clusters on the outside branches. In summer plants bear green berries that turn bright orange-red in fall and ripen for birds in mid- to late winter.

**BIRDS ATTRACTED:** Toyon fruits are particularly attractive to Cedar Waxwing, American Robin, Northern Mockingbird, Western Bluebird, Hermit Thrush, and most woodpeckers and finches.

**ALTERNATIVES:** Toyons are members of the rose family (Rosaceae) and are closely related to photinias, exotic look-alikes from China and Japan, which produce fruits that are not favored by North American birds. An East Coast holly, *Ilex opaca,* though unrelated, might be a suitable substitute.

Yellow-berried toyon, or California holly

---

*Justicia spicigera*
**MEXICAN HONEYSUCKLE**
Its easily accessible blossoms and long flowering period draw hummingbirds to this low-growing, multi-stemmed plant.

**NATIVE HABITAT:** Dry areas of the Southwest and Mexico.

**USDA HARDINESS ZONES:** 10; protection required in 9; survives in warmer microclimates in 8 and 9

**FLOWERS AND FRUIT:** Orange, upright, tubular-shaped flowers are borne in clusters on new growth. Position of the flower makes it ideal for hummingbirds and assures that it is seldom visited by carpenter bees. Flowers all year, though sporadically in winter, and profusely in spring and summer when given extra water.

**HOW TO GROW:** Grows from cuttings or

PACIFIC COAST

Mexican honeysuckle (*Justicia spicigera*) attracts hummingbirds year-round.

underground rooted stems, and can be transplanted. Unfortunately, it is a slow grower as a young plant, and so not a favorite of the commercial nursery trade. Once established, it grows at a moderate rate and is reliable year to year, requiring little care. Brief, below-freezing temperatures will kill the above-ground stem, but in well-established plants rootstock will survive and new shoots will appear in spring.

**BIRDS ATTRACTED:** A favorite of hummingbirds.

**ALTERNATIVES:** All of the justicias available through nurseries—shrimp plant (*J. brandegeàna*), *Dicliptera suberecta*, Brazilian plume flower (*J. carnea*), and chuparosa (*J. californica*)—are favored by hummingbirds.

*Morus rubra*
### RED MULBERRY

Red mulberry is native to the eastern U.S., but grows well with sufficient water in the West, where fruits of this early-flowering, round-headed shade tree appear at the height of spring migration and during the nesting period of resident birds.

**NATIVE HABITAT:** A variety of habitats throughout the eastern U.S., from open forests to floodplains.

**USDA HARDINESS ZONES:** All zones

**FLOWERS AND FRUIT:** Male and female flowers may appear on the same or separate trees. The inconspicuous flowers emerge in early spring, sometimes before the leaves. Fruits start out white to pale pink, ripening to deep, fleshy, blue-black. Birds prefer the fruits at the pale-pink stage, and show little interest in the watery, fleshy and overripe blue-black fruits.

**HOW TO GROW:** Red mulberry is very easy to find in the nursery trade in 1-gallon containers and as balled-and-burlapped specimens 10' to 12' tall. It does best in well-drained, deep, loamy soils; if planted in gravelly, rocky soils, it will require constant care. Plants need frequent watering in the dry season during the first several years.

**BIRDS ATTRACTED:** Wood Duck, quail, crows, jays, woodpeckers, thrushes,

The abundant fruits of red mulberry are valuable to many bird species.

Cedar Waxwing, House and Purple Finch, tanagers, and vireos all devour red mulberry fruits.

**ALTERNATIVES:** Caution!—White mulberry *(Morus alba),* a native of China, hybridizes with native red mulberry, compromising native strains and *should not be planted.*

---

## *Myrica californica*
### PACIFIC WAX MYRTLE

During periods of food scarcity, the fruits of Pacific wax myrtle are extremely beneficial for birds. In coastal areas, it grows as a flattened, spreading shrub; in inland valleys and canyons it becomes an upright, large shrub with many trunks.

**NATIVE HABITAT:** Coastal marshes and coastal mountain canyons from Southern California north to Washington.

**USDA HARDINESS ZONES:** 8 to 10

**FLOWERS AND FRUIT:** The spring flowers are inconspicuous and are followed by hard, nut-like, waxy purplish fruits that persist through the winter until ripe, when they are suitable for consumption by birds. Crushed leaves are strongly aromatic.

**HOW TO GROW:** An extremely attractive plant in the garden that can be pruned into a hedge or screen. Well-rooted container specimens are best for transplanting and require deep, thorough watering the first year, particularly

PACIFIC COAST

inland. First-year plants in hot, inland valleys may need shade until they become established.

**BIRDS ATTRACTED**: Pacific wax myrtle fruits are an important food for Western and Mountain Bluebird, Hermit and Varied Thrush, American Robin, mockingbirds, Northern Flicker, Tree Swallow, and towhees.

**ALTERNATIVES**: None.

---

*Populus fremontii*
## WESTERN COTTONWOOD

Western cottonwood is one of the best trees in the West for many species of birds. This large, multi-branched tree attains its best shape in full sun.

**NATIVE HABITAT**: Along streams and rivers, and around springs and seeps in open grasslands throughout the West, in most soils.

**USDA HARDINESS ZONES**: 8 to 10

**FLOWERS AND FRUIT**: Pale yellow-green flowers appear on long, slender catkins similar to those of the willow. The catkins produce small seeds attached to cottony fluff, which helps transport the seeds on windy days.

**HOW TO GROW**: Western cottonwood is a fairly easy tree to propagate from cuttings or to transplant from containers. Cuttings taken in late fall to mid-winter and pushed into the ground near permanently wet or moist areas usually take root. Trees planted from contain-

ers also do well but need frequent, thorough soakings throughout the dry, rainless summer months. Once established, with roots tapped into underground water sources, little summer water is needed. Clumps of cottonwoods serve birds best.

**BIRDS ATTRACTED**: Cedar Waxwing flocks to the tree in the spring to feed on the unopened buds of the catkins; warblers feed on small insects attracted to the flowers and the sweet sap found in the branches and leaves; and orioles, tanagers, and vireos nest among the branches and leaves. As the tree matures, woodpeckers excavate cavities for nesting in its branches.

**ALTERNATIVES**: Quaking aspen *(Populus tremuloides)* prefers moist mountain situations but will grow at lower elevations, where it is usually much shorter-lived; black cottonwood *(Populus trichocarpa)* is found along mountain streams and in the Coast Ranges near wet, boggy areas. These are similar to cottonwood in their attractiveness to birds and other wildlife.

---

*Quercus agrifolia*
## COAST LIVE OAK

Many species of western birds use the dense foliage of this live oak for feeding, nesting, and roosting. It is a widespreading but dense, round-headed tree that will grow as tall as 65'.

**NATIVE HABITAT:** Coast mountain ranges, in open, dry grasslands, and along steep slopes and canyons in well-drained soils.

**USDA HARDINESS ZONES:** 8 to 10

**FLOWERS AND FRUIT:** Flowers are inconspicuous. The dense, evergreen foliage and, in fertile years, masses of acorns benefit wildlife.

**HOW TO GROW:** Today, many native plant and commercial ornamental plant nurseries are growing this tree for homeowners as well as for oak woodland restoration. Coast live oak has deep tap roots, so look for specimens in tubular pots 12" to 20" deep or larger specimens in 5-gallon containers. Plants that are slightly pot-bound tend to do better when transplanted, as the roots are less likely to be broken or have the soil around them disturbed. Water well throughout the summer if planted in spring; less often, but frequently, if planted in the fall or winter for the first year or two. Does best in full sun.

**BIRDS ATTRACTED:** In good years, when acorn production is high, Acorn Woodpecker, Scrub Jay, Steller's Jay, Yellow-billed Magpie, Northern Flicker, Pileated Woodpecker, and Wild Turkey feast on the crop. Acorn Woodpecker and Scrub Jay store or hide huge numbers of nuts. The Scrub Jay is considered the chief planter of oak trees in the West.

**ALTERNATIVES:** Canyon live oak *(Quercus*

Male catkins of coast live oak

*chrysolepis)* and interior live oak *(Q. wislizeni)* are suitable alternatives. Canyon live oak tolerates more moisture and cooler temperatures, while interior live oak appears to be more drought-tolerant. They are both similar in attractiveness for gardens and birds.

---

*Ribes aureum*
**GOLDEN CURRANT**

Many spring migrant and resident birds consume the spring and early summer fruits of the golden currant, and resident birds feed the fruits to their hungry young. This rambling shrub grows from 4' to 12' tall.

**NATIVE HABITAT:** Meadows, fields, and

woodlands, usually within view of a spring, stream, or river in inland valleys.

**USDA HARDINESS ZONES:** All zones

**HOW TO GROW:** You'll probably find this plant more readily at a native-plant nursery, but check in ornamental commercial nurseries also. A tough, hardy species, golden currant can tolerate many soil types; it appears to do equally well in good to poor soils. Once established, plants do not require any summer water and go dormant in the hottest, driest months. New leaves and flowers appear in late January and early February.

**FLOWERS AND FRUIT:** Bright yellow flowers appear in early spring, from February to May, followed by pea-sized, red to blue-black fruits.

**BIRDS ATTRACTED:** Quail, Band-tailed Pigeon, Western Scrub Jay, Black-headed Grosbeak, Hermit and Swainson's Thrush, Plain Titmouse, and California

and Spotted Towhee, among many others, relish these fruits.

**ALTERNATIVES:** There are many suitable species of currants and gooseberries. (Gooseberries have spines while currants lack them.) Red-flowering currant *(Ribes sanguineum)* and fuchsia-flowering gooseberry of southern California *(R. speciosum)* are attractive alternatives for western gardens.

---

*Salvia leucantha*
**MEXICAN BUSH SAGE**
Mexican bush sage attracts all hummingbirds of the West. The upright or gracefully arching plant can grow to 7'.

**NATIVE HABITAT:** Central and eastern Mexico in tropical and subtropical conifer forests.

**USDA HARDINESS ZONES:** 8 to 10; can be grown as an annual in colder zones.

**FLOWERS AND FRUIT:** Mexican bush sage has long, erect or slightly arching velvet spikes of white, purple, or pink flowers; spikes produce blooms for long periods. New plants begin blooming in October and November; older, established specimens that have not been cut back may bloom sporadically through spring and summer.

**HOW TO GROW:** Grows well in deep, loamy soils as well as gravelly, sandy soils. Established plants do not transplant well. Container-grown plants transplant easily and do well. Appears

Golden currant (*Ribes aureum*)

Mexican bush sage

to prefer dry summers with occasional watering.

**BIRDS ATTRACTED:** A favorite for Anna's Hummingbirds overwintering in northern California to coastal Oregon and Washington, but will attract all of the western species.

**ALTERNATIVES:** Salvias are increasing in popularity, and vary widely in color and growth habit. Almost all are visited by hummingbirds.

*Sambucus mexicana*
### MEXICAN ELDERBERRY
The most widespread of several species of *Sambucus*, Mexican elderberry has a long flowering and fruiting period, so it is visited by many species of birds. This medium-sized to large, branching, spreading shrub thrives in what would be harsh, dry conditions for most elderberries, and can grow to 30'.

**NATIVE HABITAT:** Dry uplands, but usually within sight of a stream, creek, river, seep, or spring.

**USDA HARDINESS ZONES:** 7 to 10

**FLOWERS AND FRUIT:** Creamy to white flowers are borne on large, flat-topped clusters from 2" to 10" across, from April to September. They are a favorite of bees and other insects. The fruits are deep purple to blue-black, and turn silvery if not consumed immediately by birds. Because of the plant's long flowering period, berries are present throughout the summer.

**HOW TO GROW:** You will generally find the best specimens in native plant nurseries, in everything from long tubes to 5-gallon containers. Plants transplant easily from tubes or pots and need thorough watering the first year. They prefer deep, loamy soil and will not do well in soil that remains saturated for long periods of time; with too much water, they will get leggy and spindly.

**BIRDS ATTRACTED:** A favorite of Northern Mockingbird, American Robin, Cedar Waxwing, Black-headed Grosbeak, Western Tanager, Yellow-breasted Chat, Bullock's Oriole, House Finch, Wild Turkey, quail, and most of the western woodpeckers.

PACIFIC COAST

ALTERNATIVES: While *S. mexicana* does best in lowland gardens, blue elderberry *(S. caerulea)*, does better at high elevations along moving water courses. It goes by several other botanical names, including *S. glauca.*

## MORE GREAT BIRD PLANTS FOR THE PACIFIC COAST

*Trees*

American Persimmon *(Diospyros virginiana)* zones 8 to 10

Box Elder *(Acer negundo)* zones 7 to 10

California Sycamore *(Platanus racemosa)* zones 8 to 1

Mountain Ash *(Sorbus scopulina)* zones 7 to 10

Oregon Ash *(Fraxinus latifolia)* zones 8 to 10

Western Hawthorn *(Crataegus douglasii)* zones 7 to 10

Western Red Cedar *(Thuja plicata)* zones 7 to 10

Western Redbud *(Cercis occidentalis)* zones 7 and 8

Western Serviceberry *(Amelanchier alnifolia)* zones 7 to 9

*Shrubs*

Hollyleaf Cherry *( Prunus ilicifolia)* zones 9 and 10

Huckleberries *(Vaccinium* species) zones vary according to species

Longleaf Mahonia *(Mahonia nervosa)* zones 8 to 10

Manzanitas *(Arctostaphylos* species) zones vary according to species

*Vines*

Twinberry *(Lonicera involucrata)* zones 8 to 10

Western Clematis *(Clematis ligustici-folia)* zones 8 to 10

Wild Grape *(Vitis californica)* zones 8 to 10

*Hummingbird Plants*

Cardinal Flower *(Lobelia cardinalis* subsp. *graminea)* zones 7 to 10

Common Beardtongue *(Penstemon barbatus)* zones 7 to 10

Fuchsia-flowering Gooseberry *(Ribes speciosum)* zones 9 and 10

Pineapple Sage *(Salvia elegans)* zone 10; in 8 and 9 can be grown as an annual

Sky Lupine *(Lupinus nanus)* zones 8 to 10

Yellow Monkey Flower *(Mimulus guttatus)* zones 8 to 10

Anna's Hummingbird is one of several hummingbird species in the West.

PACIFIC COAST

The following lists include birds often found in backyard habitats, both resident species and common migrants. They also include some "irruptive" species (designated with "I"), such as Pine Siskin and Red Crossbill, which occur frequently in some winters, but are rare in others. In addition to the species listed here, hundreds of others fly over or visit backyards during migration. To help with identifications and to learn which species are most likely to visit your backyard, consult a field guide to birds. For the purpose of this book, North American birds are divided into eastern and western birds, using as the dividing line the 100th meridian, which runs from central North Dakota, south through central Texas, to the Gulf of Mexico. Listed species are common throughout the region at the proper season, except for those that are common only in subregions, which are noted by the following designations: NE (Northeast), SE (Southeast), SF (South Florida), PP (prairies and plains), M&D (mountains and deserts), and PC (Pacific Coast).

## EASTERN BIRDS

Sharp-shinned Hawk
Cooper's Hawk
Northern Bobwhite
Eastern Screech-owl
Great Horned Owl
Mourning Dove
Common Ground-Dove, SE
Chimney Swift
Ruby-throated Hummingbird
Downy Woodpecker
Hairy Woodpecker
Yellow-bellied Sapsucker
Red-bellied Woodpecker
Red-headed Woodpecker
Northern Flicker
Pileated Woodpecker
Eastern Phoebe
Eastern Wood-pewee
Great-crested Flycatcher
Eastern Kingbird
Purple Martin

Tree Swallow
Barn Swallow
Cliff Swallow
Blue Jay
American Crow
Fish Crow, SE
Black-capped Chickadee
Carolina Chickadee, SE
Tufted Titmouse
Red-breasted Nuthatch
White-breasted Nuthatch
Brown-headed Nuthatch, SE
Brown Creeper
Carolina Wren
House Wren
Golden-crowned Kinglet
Ruby-crowned Kinglet
Blue-gray Gnatcatcher
Eastern Bluebird
Veery
Hermit Thrush
Wood Thrush

Cedar Waxwing on gray dogwood

American Robin
Gray Catbird
Northern Mockingbird
Brown Thrasher
Cedar Waxwing
European Starling
Red-eyed Vireo
Blue-headed Vireo
Yellow-throated Vireo
Warbling Vireo
Yellow Warbler
Chestnut-sided Warbler
Yellow-rumped Warbler
Common Yellowthroat
American Redstart
Ovenbird

American Tree Sparrow

Common Yellowthroat
Scarlet Tanager
Summer Tanager, SE
Northern Cardinal
Rose-breasted Grosbeak
Indigo Bunting
Painted Bunting, SE
Blue Grosbeak, SE
Eastern Towhee
American Tree Sparrow, NE
Chipping Sparrow
Field Sparrow
Fox Sparrow
Song Sparrow
Swamp Sparrow
White-throated Sparrow
White-crowned Sparrow
Dark-eyed Junco, NE
Common Grackle
Boat-tailed Grackle, SE

Brown-headed Cowbird
Red-winged Blackbird
Baltimore Oriole
Orchard Oriole, SE, PP
Pine Grosbeak, NE, PP
Purple Finch, I
House Finch
Red Crossbill, I, NE
White-winged Crossbill, I, NE
Common Redpoll, I, NE
Pine Siskin, I, NE
American Goldfinch
Evening Grosbeak, I, NE, PP
House Sparrow

**WESTERN BIRDS**
Sharp-shinned Hawk
Cooper's Hawk
California Quail, PC
Gambel's Quail, M&D

Western Screech-owl
Black-chinned Hummingbird
Anna's Hummingbird, PC
Broad-tailed Hummingbird,
   M&D
Rufous Hummingbird
Allen's Hummingbird, PC
Chimney Swift
Lewis's Woodpecker, M&D
Nuttall's Woodpecker, PC,
   M&D
Acorn Woodpecker, PC, M&D
Red-naped Sapsucker, M&D
Red-breasted Sapsucker, PC
Ladder-backed Woodpecker,
   M&D
Downy Woodpecker
Hairy Woodpecker
Northern Flicker
Pileated Woodpecker

Black Phoebe

Say's Phoebe

Ash-throated Flycatcher

Western Kingbird

Tree Swallow

Violet-green Swallow

Cliff Swallow

Barn Swallow

Gray Jay

Steller's Jay

Western Scrub Jay

Pinyon Jay, M&D

Clark's Nutcracker, M&D

Black-billed Magpie, M&D

Yellow-billed Magpie, PC

American Crow

Black-capped Chickadee, M&D

Mountain Chickadee, M&D

Chestnut-backed Chickadee, PC

Oak Titmouse, PC

Juniper Titmouse, M&D

Verdin, M&D

Bushtit

Red-breasted Nuthatch

White-breasted Nuthatch

Pygmy Nuthatch, M&D

Brown Creeper

Rock Wren

Canyon Wren

Bewick's Wren

House Wren

Winter Wren, PC

Golden-crowned Kinglet

Ruby-crowned Kinglet

Blue-gray Gnatcatcher

Western Bluebird

Mountain Bluebird, M&D

Townsend's Solitaire, M&D

Swainson's Thrush

Hermit Thrush

American Robin

Varied Thrush, PC

Wrentit, PC

Gray Catbird, M&D

Northern Mockingbird

Sage Thrasher, M&D

California Thrasher, PC

Curve-billed Thrasher, M&D

Bendire's Thrasher, M&D

Cedar Waxwing

Phainopepla, M&D

European Starling

Warbling Vireo

Orange-crowned Warbler

Yellow Warbler

Nashville Warbler

Yellow-rumped Warbler

Townsend's Warbler

Black-throated Gray Warbler

Common Yellowthroat

Wilson's Warbler

Yellow-breasted Chat

Western Tanager

Pyrrhuloxia, M&D

Black-headed Grosbeak

Lazuli Bunting

Green-tailed Towhee, M&D

Spotted Towhee, M&D, PC

California Towhee, PC

Canyon Towhee, M&D

American Tree Sparrow, PP

Chipping Sparrow

Vesper Sparrow

Lark Sparrow

Lark Bunting, M&D

Fox Sparrow

Song Sparrow

Lincoln's Sparrow

Swamp Sparrow

White-crowned Sparrow

Golden-crowned Sparrow

White-throated Sparrow

Harris's Sparrow, PP

Dark-eyed Junco

Red-winged Blackbird

Yellow-headed Blackbird

Brewer's Blackbird

Great-tailed Grackle

Common Grackle, PP

Brown-headed Cowbird

Bullock's Oriole

Hooded Oriole, M&D, PC

Scott's Oriole, M&D

Pine Grosbeak, I, M&D

Purple Finch, M&D, PC

Cassin's Finch, M&D

House Finch

Red Crossbill, I, M&D, PC

Common Redpoll, I, M&D, PC

Pine Siskin, I

Lesser Goldfinch

Lawrence's Goldfinch, PC

American Goldfinch

Evening Grosbeak, I, M&D

House Sparrow

*The following mail-order suppliers offer a good selection of native plants.*

Ruby-throated Hummingbird on trumpet creeper

## NORTHEAST

**Bergeson Nursery**
Route 1, Box 184
Fertile, MN 56540
(218) 945-6988

**Kurt Bluemel, Inc.**
2740 Greene Lane
Baldwin, MD 21013
(410) 557-7229

**Carroll Gardens**
444 East Main Street
PO Box 310
Westminister, MD 21158
(410) 848-5422

**Wild Earth Native Plant Nursery**
49 Mead Avenue
Freehold, NJ 07728
(908) 308-9777

**Wildlife Nurseries, Inc.**
PO Box 2724
Oshkosh, WI 54903-2724
(920) 231-3780

## SOUTHEAST AND SOUTH FLORIDA

**Apalachee Native Nursery**
Eric Jadaszewski
Route 3, Box 156
Monticello, FL 32344
(904) 997-8976

**Environmental Equities**
Michael Kenton
PO Box 7180
Hudson, FL 34674-7180
(941) 355-1267
envequity@aol.com

**Green Images**
David Drylie
1333 Taylor Creek Road
Christmas, FL 32709
(407) 568-1333
(407) 568-2061 (fax)
greenimage@aol.com

**Liner Farm, Inc.**
David Biggar
PO Box 701369
St. Cloud, FL 34770-1369
(800) 330-1484
(407) 892-3593 (fax)
*Sells plants only in quantities greater than 100*

**The Natives**
Nancy Bissett
2929 J.B. Carter Road
Davenport, FL 33837

(941) 422-6664
(941) 421-6520 (fax)
natives@gate.net

**Superior Trees, Inc.**
Alan Webb
PO Box 9325
Lee, FL 32059
(904) 971-5159

## PRAIRIES AND PLAINS

**Clear Creek Farms**
PO Box 89
Peggs, OK 74452
(918) 598-3782

**Missouri Wildflowers Nursery**
9814 Pleasant Hill Road
Jefferson City, MO 65109
(573) 496-3492

**Prairie Hill Wildflowers**
8955 Lemond Road
Ellendale, MN 56026
(507) 451-7791

**Prairie Nursery**
PO Box 306
Westfield, WI 53964
(800) 476-9453

**Prairie Restorations**
PO Box 327
Princeton, MN 55371
(612) 389-4342

**Rock Post Wildflowers**
5798 Windy Meadows Lane
Fulton, MO 65251
(573) 642-6927

**Sunshine Nursery**
Route 1, Box 4030
Clinton, OK 73601
(405) 323-6259

**Walker's Green Space**
2699 53rd Street
Vinton, IA 52349
(800) 837-3873

**PACIFIC COAST,
MOUNTAINS & DESERTS**

**Cornflower Farms**
PO Box 896
Elk Grove, CA 95759
(916) 689-1015
*Wholesale only*

**Forestfarm**
990 Tetherow Road
Williams, OR 97544
(541) 846-7269

**Mockingbird Nursery**
1670 Jackson Street
Riverside, CA 92505
(909) 780-3571

**Tree of Life Nursery**
P.O. Box 635
33201 Ortega Highway
San Juan Capistrano, CA
92693
(714) 728-0685
*Wholesale nursery that is
open to the public on Fri-
days and some Saturdays*

**SOURCE DIRECTORIES**

*The following directories
list the plants found in this
handbook and where to
obtain them.*

**Andersen Horticultural
Library's Source List of
Plants and Seeds**
AHL, Minnesota Land-
scape Arboretum
3675 Arboretum Drive
Box 39
Chanhassen, MN 55317
(612) 443-2440

**Hortus Northwest**
PO Box 955
Canby, OR 97013

**New England Wild
Flower Society**
Garden in the Woods
180 Hemenway Road
Framingham, MA 01701
(508) 877-7630
*Publishes a list of suppliers
that offer nursery-propagat-
ed (as opposed to wild-col-
lected) native plants*

**Florida Native
Nurseries**
PO Box 436
Melrose, FL 32666
(800) 293-5413

**Nursery Sources for
California Native Plants**
Department of Conservation
Division of Mines and
    Geology Library
Mail Stop 14-34
Sacramento, CA 95814
(916) 445-5716
*Printed in 1995 and
includes nurseries in
Washington and Oregon.
Request "DMG open-file
report 90-04."*

**Where on Earth: A
Guide to Specialty
Nurseries and Other
Resources for California
Gardeners**; 1997; Stevens,
Barbara and Nancy Con-
nor; Heyday Books, Berke-
ley, California.

**The National Wild-
flower Research Center**
in Austin, Texas, publishes up-to-date lists of native
plant sources throughout
the U.S. For information
on sources in your state,
call the Center's clearing-
house at (512) 292-1702.

## FURTHER READING

Bormann, Herman, Diana Balmori, and Gordon T. Begalle, 1993. *Redesigning the American Lawn—A Search for Environmental Harmony,* Yale University Press, New Haven

Kress, Stephen W., 1984. *The Audubon Society Guide to Attracting Birds.* New York: Macmillan Publishing Co.

Kress, Stephen W., 1995. *The Audubon Society Bird Garden.* New York: Dorling Kindersley

Martin, Alexander C, Herbert S. Zim, and Arnold L. Nelson, 1961. *American Wildlife and Plants: A Guide to Wildlife Food Habits.* New York: Dover Publications, Inc.

Newfield, Nancy L. and Barbara Nielsen, 1996. *Hummingbird Gardens.* Shelburne, Vermont: Chapters Publishing, Ltd.

Scott, Virgil E., Keith E. Evans, David R. Patton, and Charles P. Stoe, 1977. *Cavity-Nesting Birds of North American Forests.* Washington, DC: USDA Forest Service Agriculture Handbook 511

Stokes, Donald and Lillian, 1990. *The Complete Birdhouse Book.* Boston: Little, Brown and Co.

Terres, John K, 1994. *Songbirds in Your Garden.* Chapel Hill, North Carolina: Algonquin Books

McKenny, Margaret, 1939. *Birds in the Garden and How to Attract Them.* New York: Reynal and Hitchcock

Zeleny, Lawrence, 1976. *The Bluebird.* Bloomington: Indiana University Press

## ORGANIZATIONS

*The following organizations can provide additional information about landscaping for birds and bird conservation:*

Cornell Laboratory of Ornithology
159 Sapsucker Woods Road
Ithaca, NY 14850

National Audubon Society
700 Broadway
New York, NY 10003

National Wildlife Federation
8925 Leesburg Pike
Vienna, VA 22184

## JESSE GRANTHAM

Jesse Grantham is a biologist with the National Audubon Society in Sacramento, California, where he is the director of the Society's western sanctuaries. He has extensive experience in horticulture, habitat restoration, and wildlife management. He writes and lectures throughout the country on gardening for wildlife.

## MAUREEN KUWANO HINKLE

Maureen Kuwano Hinkle directs the agricultural policy program for the National Audubon Society, where she has worked since 1981; before that, she worked for the Environmental Defense Fund on pesticide issues.

## BETH HUNING

Beth Huning is the director of Richardson Bay Audubon Center and Sanctuary. She directs education and wildlife conservation programs at the 900-acre water-bird sanctuary and environmental education center on San Francisco Bay. She coordinates the development of demonstration landscape gardens, bird-feeding stations, and wildlife habitat programs.

## STEPHEN W. KRESS

Stephen W. Kress is director of the National Audubon Society's Seabird Restoration Program and manager of the Society's Maine coast seabird sanctuaries. He teaches field ornithology courses at the Cornell Laboratory of Ornithology, where he is a research associate. He is author of *The Audubon Society Bird Garden, The Audubon Society Guide to Attracting Birds,* the Golden Guide *Bird Life,* and other publications on birds and their management.

## DANIEL M. SAVERCOOL

Daniel M. Savercool is an ecologist with Dames and Moore in Tampa, Florida. He has over 14 years experience in habitat management, specializing in coastal and inland wetlands and uplands in the Southeast. He is active in several environmental organizations, and currently serves as the president of the Tampa Audubon Society.

## RICHARD THOM

Richard Thom has a lifelong interest in birds, native plants, gardening, and wildlife habitat. He has worked as a biologist for the National Audubon Society, the Illinois Nature Preserves Commission, and the Missouri Department of Conservation, where he currently serves as chief of the Natural History Section. Rick and his family live on five acres of hilly land near Jefferson City, Missouri, which they have thoroughly bird-scaped over the past ten years.

**ILLUSTRATION CREDITS:**

STEVE BUCHANAN, map, page 106

R. & S. DAY/VIREO, page 1

SUSAN M. GLASCOCK, pages 27, 29, 46, 52, 60, 66, 68, 79

JESSE GRANTHAM, pages 90, 91

W. GREENE/VIREO, page 35

ROGER HAMMER, pages 44, 51, 53, 54, 55, 56

PAMELA HARPER, page 41, 58

JOHN HEIDECKER for the Cornell Laboratory of Ornithology, page 10

MIKE HOPIAK for the Cornell Laboratory of Ornithology, page 101

ISIDOR JEKLIN for the Cornell Laboratory of Ornithology, cover, pages 6, 18, 99

STEPHEN W. KRESS, pages 12 (bottom), 28, 30, 33, 36, 98

CHARLES MANN, pages 14, 16, 75, 76, 78, 80, 82, 83, 85

JERRY PAVIA, pages 12 (top), 32, 81, 89, 95

BOB PERRY, pages 86, 87, 88, 93, 94

B. RANDALL/VIREO, page 9

C. R. SAMS II & J. F. STOICK, page 13

DANIEL M. SAVERCOOL, pages 39, 42, 43, 57, 59

B. SCHORRE/VIREO, page 5

JOHANN SCHUMACHER/VIREO, pages 8, 45, 71

H. P. SMITH, JR./VIREO, pages 17, 97

RICHARD THOM, pages 21, 26, 38, 63, 64, 65, 67, 69, 70, 72

T. VEZO/VIREO, page 61

J. ROBERT WOODWARD for the Cornell Laboratory of Ornithology, page 49

# HARDINESS ZONE MAP

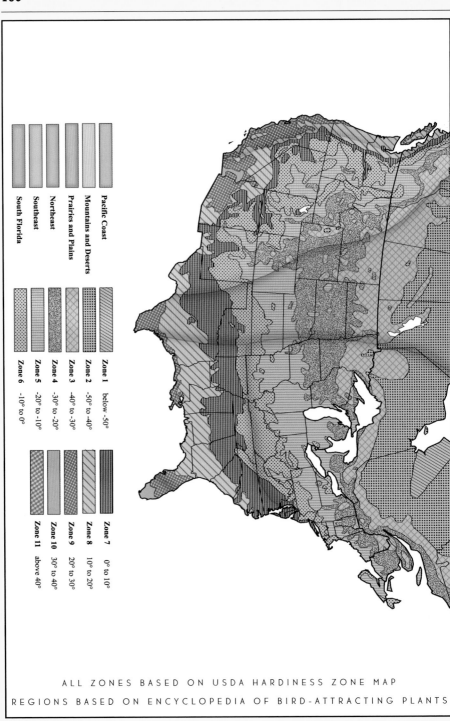

**Pacific Coast**

**Mountains and Deserts**

**Prairies and Plains**

**Northeast**

**Southeast**

**South Florida**

| | |
|---|---|
| **Zone 1** | below -50° |
| **Zone 2** | -50° to -40° |
| **Zone 3** | -40° to -30° |
| **Zone 4** | -30° to -20° |
| **Zone 5** | -20° to -10° |
| **Zone 6** | -10° to 0° |
| **Zone 7** | 0° to 10° |
| **Zone 8** | 10° to 20° |
| **Zone 9** | 20° to 30° |
| **Zone 10** | 30° to 40° |
| **Zone 11** | above 40° |

ALL ZONES BASED ON USDA HARDINESS ZONE MAP

REGIONS BASED ON ENCYCLOPEDIA OF BIRD-ATTRACTING PLANTS

# INDEX

# BROOKLYN BOTANIC GARDEN

## 21 ST-CENTURY GARDENING SERIES

for further information please contact the

**BROOKLYN BOTANIC GARDEN**

1000 Washington Avenue

Brooklyn, New York 11225

(718) 622-4433 ext. 265  www.bbg.org